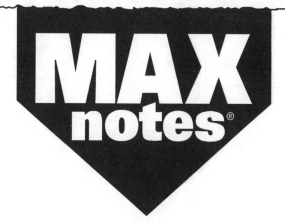

Arthur Miller's

The
Crucible

Text by
Beth L. Tanis
*(M.A., University of
North Carolina at Chapel Hill)*

*Illustrati
Karen

D1364965

Research & Education Association

Dr. M. Fogiel, Director

MAXnotes® for
THE CRUCIBLE

Printed in the United States of America

Library of Congress Control Number 2001098090

International Standard Book Number 0-87891-753-5

MAXnotes® is a registered trademark of
Research & Education Association, Piscataway, New Jersey 08854

What **MAXnotes**® *Will Do for You*

This book is intended to help you absorb the essential contents and features of Arthur Miller's *The Crucible* and to help you gain a thorough understanding of the work. Our book has been designed to do this more quickly and effectively than any other study guide.

For best results, this **MAXnotes** book should be used as a companion to the actual work, not instead of it. The interaction between the two will greatly benefit you.

To help you in your studies, this book presents the most up-to-date interpretations of every section of the actual work, followed by questions and fully explained answers that will enable you to analyze the material critically. The questions also will help you to test your understanding of the work and will prepare you for discussions and exams.

Meaningful illustrations are included to further enhance your understanding and enjoyment of the literary work. The illustrations are designed to place you into the mood and spirit of the work's settings.

The **MAXnotes** also include summaries, character lists, explanations of plot, and section-by-section analyses. A biography of the author and discussion of the work's historical context will help you put this literary piece into the proper framework of what is taking place.

The use of this study guide will save you the hours of preparation time that would ordinarily be required to arrive at a complete grasp of this work of literature. You will be well-prepared for classroom discussions, homework, and exams. The guidelines that are included for writing papers and reports on various topics will prepare you for any added work which may be assigned.

The **MAXnotes** will take your grades "to the max."

Dr. Max Fogiel
Program Director

Contents

> **Each Scene Includes List of Characters,
> Summary, Analysis, Study Questions and
> Answers, and Suggested Essay Topics.**

A Glance at Some of the Characters

Samuel Parris

Betty Parris

Abigail Williams

John Proctor

Elizabeth Proctor

John Hale

Ezekiel Cheever

Tituba

Introduction

The Life and Work of Arthur Miller

Arthur Miller is considered, along with Tennessee Williams and Eugene O'Neill, to be one of America's greatest playwrights. He was born on October 17, 1915, in New York City. Miller's father was in the clothing business and was hit hard by the Depression. In 1934 Miller entered the University of Michigan, Ann Arbor, to study journalism. His first play, *Honors at Dawn*, was produced in 1936 while he was a student there. The play received the first of a string of awards, the Hopwood Award for Drama in 1937.

After graduating from the University of Michigan, Miller began working with the Federal Theatre Project. He married Mary Grace Slattery in 1940. After writing several plays and a novel, he won the New York Drama Critics' Circle Award in 1947 for *All My Sons*. This success was followed two years later by *Death of a Salesman*, which won a Pulitzer Prize and the New York Drama Critics' Circle Award in 1949. This drama, which deals with the unrealized dreams and hopes of an ordinary man, was the most popularly successful of all Arthur Miller's plays and set the standard for all his subsequent work.

The Crucible was produced and published in 1953. Judged against the standard of *Salesman*, the play was found wanting. Critics wrote that it lacked the depth and intellectual insight of the earlier play and that the characters did not seem fully human. Still it was praised for commenting on the current political climate of fervent anti-communism without heavy-handed preaching and fingerpointing. The play fared better when it was revived off

Broadway some years later—after the political situation had changed—and is today considered one of the finest plays written in America.

In 1954, the State Department refused to issue Miller a passport to attend the opening of *The Crucible* in Brussels. In 1956 he was called before the House Un-American Activities Committee to answer charges that he held Communist sympathies. He admitted that he had attended a meeting of Communist writers, but denied ever being a member of the Communist party. That same year he also divorced Mary Slattery and married Marilyn Monroe. The following year, he was convicted of contempt of Congress for refusing to name other suspected Communists. The conviction was reversed by the Supreme Court in 1958.

In 1958 Miller was also elected to the National Arts and Letters Institute. In 1961 he divorced Marilyn Monroe and married his third wife, Ingeborg Morath, the following year. The couple had a daughter, Rebecca Augusta Miller, the same year. In 1965 Miller was elected the International President of PEN, the highly prestigious Poets, Essayists, and Novelists association. He continued to publish and produce plays until 1982.

Historical Background

Arthur Miller's writing spans a large block of twentieth-century American history. He was certainly influenced by the effects of the Great Depression, which uprooted his family when he was in his early teens. Anyone who lived through the deprivation and despair of the Depression could not help but be touched by it. Much of that despair is evident in *Death of a Salesman*, as the protagonist struggles to make ends meet.

Salesman was also highly influenced by the idea of the "American Dream" that was so pervasive in the early 1950s. After World War II there was a tremendous growth in the country's economy. Many Americans were able to pull themselves out of relative poverty through hard work and determination. There was a contagious optimism and a feeling that anything was possible. Children were financially better off than their parents had been, and there was no end in sight to the continuation of prosperity. Still, there were those who were not so successful; those who did not manage to grasp a piece of the American Dream. For them, the failure was magnified by the success they saw around them.

Arguably, the historical context central to *The Crucible* is the "Red Terror" of the 1950s. When China fell to the Communists, many intellectuals in the United States began to ask questions. The government could not afford challenges to its authority. A fervent hunt for suspected Communist sympathizers ensued, led by Senator Joseph McCarthy. McCarthy, a colorful and clever speaker, claimed that Communists had infiltrated government offices and succeeded in driving many people out of their jobs. Even those who were not found to be Communists were permanently tainted in public opinion by McCarthy's accusations. Many were added to blacklists, which barred certain actors and writers from working. Those who refused to testify could no longer find work, while those who cooperated continued to work. As part of the hunt, Clifford Odets was brought before McCarthy and confessed to being a Communist. He was persuaded to name names of others he knew to be Communists, and he pointed to director Elia Kazan. Kazan, in turn, confessed and named names, among which was Arthur Miller.

"McCarthyism," as it has come to be called, was a particularly shameful chapter of American history. Many citizens were accused with little or no evidence, and their lives were permanently disrupted by the stigma of having been involved. The country was thrown into a mass hysteria similar to that of the witch trials at the center of *The Crucible*. The effect is a clear and disturbing picture of history repeating itself. Just as many innocent lives were taken in the late 1600s in Salem, Massachusetts, so the reputations of many innocent people were tarnished in the late 1950s in America. Miller himself denies that his play was written as a direct response to the political situation of his time. The parallel, however, is unmistakable. The real message, perhaps, is that such atrocities can occur in any age. Man will never learn from his mistakes.

Salem and Puritanism

The government of Salem in 1692 was a Puritan theocracy. In other words, the town was under the unbending authority of the church. The leaders of the church, and especially the minister of the church, were very powerful figures, comparable to our elected officials. A person who was not a member in good standing of the church was not allowed to live in the community. All citizens were expected to conform to the teachings of the church at all times and to know its catechism, which contained the written statements of the church's beliefs.

Puritan theology was largely based on the teachings of John Calvin. Calvin was one of a group of theologians who protested against the Roman Catholic church's departure from the Bible as the ultimate authority. Based on their reading of Saint Paul in the New Testament, they particularly disagreed with the Roman Catholic emphasis on earning your salvation through good deeds on earth. These protesters, or Protestants, believed that salvation could not be earned. The only way to get to heaven was to be chosen by God and to have faith that He would save you from eternal damnation. Some people were predestined, or chosen to be saved, while others were not. While good works would not earn your salvation if you had not been chosen, believers desired to do good works on earth and thus follow the example set by Jesus Christ. Good works were visible signs of your commitment to God.

At the time of the Reformation, most of Europe was ruled by a theocracy of its own; that of the Roman Catholic church. The Protestants were compelled by their beliefs to disregard many of the practices of the Catholic church, including buying indulgences and approaching God only through a priest. The church was not pleased with this rebellion against its authority, and the Protestants were greatly persecuted. Many of them left Europe and settled in America to escape this persecution and practice their religion in peace. This was the case with the colony at Salem.

Miller himself has asserted that the community created by such a system was crucial to the survival of the colony against great odds. The settlers of Salem had to deal with attacks from Indians, harsh winters, unyielding soil, and many other hardships. Similar colonies that were not bound by common ideology eventually failed; the Virginia Colony is a good example. In contrast, the people of Salem were united in the strong bonds of a persecuted minority. Their religion required them to act honorably towards their fellow men and to help each other. They were expected to meet regularly at the Meeting House. A strong work ethic was also part of their theology. All of these things contributed to their survival.

Despite the advantages of such a system, however, *The Crucible* vividly shows it can lead to the loss of any sense of proportion. The Puritans had taken Calvinist theology several steps beyond what Calvin had in mind. While a man's good deeds could not earn him salvation, they were often used in Salem to determine the quality of his religious life and thus his standings in the community. While Calvin asserted that each man was responsible for his own salvation, the Puritans often took it upon themselves to determine the state of another man's soul. There was a great emphasis on avoiding damnation, and public confession and "coming back to God" after sin was actively encouraged. Given the importance of good deeds and hard work, as well as the harsh conditions of life in early America, there was little time for pleasure. Many of the pleasures we take for granted, such as dancing, were deemed frivolous and were not permitted. Every facet of life was touched by the rigid teachings of the church, which were strictly enforced. Failure to conform met with harsh penalties, the most severe of which was death by hanging.

Just as the Catholic church had persecuted the Protestants for failing to conform to their rules, so the Protestants persecuted those who did not conform to theirs. There was no room in Salem for free speech. The Bible was the only authority that was recognized, and any teaching not found there was considered not only false, but dangerous. Espousing views not taught by the Bible could lead others away from God, and thus imperil many souls, not just one. Witchcraft was especially dangerous, as its goal was to draw people away from God and into conspiracy with the devil. It was not, however, the only sin punishable by death in Salem. Evidence shows that many who confessed to be Quakers were also hanged. The Puritans would not tolerate even the discussion of an idea contrary to their belief system. It was this atmosphere of repression and fear of punishment that ultimately led to the mass hysteria of the Salem Witch Trials. In short, the system became so important as to completely overrule reason.

Master List of Characters

Reverend Samuel Parris—*Minister of Salem, who is not popular with everyone in town. He gave up a prosperous business in Barbados to become a minister.*

Betty Parris—*Reverend Parris' daughter and an accuser in the court*

Tituba—*slave of Reverend Parris brought back by him from Barbados*

Abigail Williams—*niece of Reverend Parris and former servant of the Proctors. Parris took her in after her parents were murdered by Indians in a raid.*

Susanna Walcott—*an accuser in the court*

Ann Putnam—*a town busybody who spreads the rumors of witchcraft*

Thomas Putnam—*husband of Ann and a prosperous landowner*

Mercy Lewis—*servant of the Putnam's and an accuser in the court*

Mary Warren—*servant of the Proctor's and an accuser in the court*

John Proctor—*husband of Elizabeth and a prominent Salem farmer*

Rebecca Nurse—*wife of Francis, accused of being a witch*

Giles Corey—*a landowner of Salem who tries to save his wife, who is accused*

Reverend John Hale—*a minister from the Boston area who is summoned to determine if there is witchcraft in Salem.*

Elizabeth Proctor—*John's wife, accused by Abigail of being a witch*

Francis Nurse—*husband of Rebecca, who tries to save her after she is accused of murder*

Ezekiel Cheever—*an employee of the court who serves arrest warrants*

Marshal Herrick—*a marshal of the court*

Judge Hathorne—*a judge of the court*

Deputy Governor Danforth—*head of the court investigation of those accused of witchcraft*

Sarah Good—*a beggar woman accused of witchcraft*

Hopkins—*a prison guard*

Summary of the Play

A group of teenage girls from Salem, Massachusetts, is discovered dancing naked in the woods by the town minister. Knowing that the punishment for their behavior will be severe, the girls claim that they were possessed by the spirits of members of the community who are trying to initiate them into witchcraft. Because of the gravity of the accusations (witchcraft is punishable by hanging), a court is set up to determine the guilt or innocence of those accused. Judges are sent to Salem from the Boston area to hear the cases. As each case is heard, the girls scream and faint to indicate whether the accused is afflicting them.

While at first only a handful of citizens are indicated, the number soon grows to over a hundred. The children, quite suspiciously, have prior grievances against many of those accused, who had in some way offended them or made their lives miserable. Abigail Williams, the niece of Salem's minister, accuses her previous employer, Elizabeth Proctor. Abigail was dismissed from her duties as the Proctor's servant when Elizabeth discovered that her husband and Abigail were having an affair. As the town of Salem is overtaken by mass hysteria, John Proctor knows from Abigail's own admission that the charges are false. He fights not only to save his wife, but also for the truth and for reason.

Elizabeth Proctor is not sentenced to hang because it is found that she is pregnant; however, John Proctor's attempts to uncover the truth bring dire consequences. Proctor brings to the judges one of the original accusers, Mary Warren, who admits that the entire group of girls is faking their "fits." This, of course, threatens to undermine the entire court, and the girls are summoned for questioning. The girls, led by Abigail, deny the charges. In a desperate attempt to discredit Abigail as a witness, Proctor then admits his adultery; however, when his wife is brought in to verify the story, she tries to save his reputation by denying the affair. Terrified of the other girls and of the punishment for lying to the court, Mary Warren soon turns against Proctor. She accuses him of being aligned with the devil and afflicting her.

While many of those found guilty of witchcraft avoid hanging by confessing a connection to the devil, 19 others are hanged. On the day that John Proctor and Rebecca Nurse, another innocent victim with high standing in Salem, are to hang, many attempts are made to coerce them to confess and save their lives. Proctor knows that he has sinned in the past and feels unworthy to die now as a saint or martyr. Thinking of his three children and of his wife, he chooses to sign a confession; however, he immediately regrets his decision and refuses to give up the paper. He cannot bear the knowledge that his signature will be used to condemn other innocent citizens. He tears up his confession, and the play closes with Elizabeth Proctor's reaction to deaths.

Estimated Reading Time

As a play, *The Crucible* was designed to be performed in one sitting. Hence, it should take you no longer than three to four hours to read it in its entirety. The play is broken up into four acts, and some editions also include an appendix, which is meant to follow Act Two. Arthur Miller himself, however, removed this scene after the original production, and it is now rarely included in performance. The appendix will not be discussed in these notes. Also, each act has been broken down into "scenes" and given titles to facilitate comprehension of the work. These divisions were incorporated into this MAXnotes and do not appear in the actual play.

Act I

(An Overture)

Scene I: Setting the Scene

New Characters:

Reverend Samuel Parris: *minister of Salem who is not popular with everyone in town. He gave up a prosperous business in Barbados to become a minister.*

Betty Parris: *Reverend Parris' daughter and an accuser in the court*

Tituba: *slave of Reverend Parris. She is from Barbados and practices island rituals.*

Abigail Williams: *niece of Reverend Parris. Parris took her in after her parents were murdered by Indians in a raid.*

Susanna Walcott: *an accuser in the court*

Ann Putnam: *townswoman who spreads the rumors of witchcraft*

Thomas Putnam: *husband of Ann and a prosperous landowner*

Mercy Lewis: *servant of the Putnam's and an accuser in the court*

Mary Warren: *an accuser in the court, and servant of the Proctors*

Summary

The play begins with a narrative section that introduces Reverend Parris and discusses life in Salem at the time the events took place. Act One opens in the bedroom of Betty Parris, daughter of Reverend Samuel Parris, minister of Salem. It is the spring of 1692. The curtain rises on Reverend Parris on his knees by his daughter's bed, in prayer. Betty herself lies motionless in her bed. As more characters come and go from the stage and speak with Reverend Parris, the events of the previous night are slowly revealed. We learn that several of the teenage girls of Salem were caught dancing naked in the woods with Tituba, Parris' slave from Barbados. The girls were discovered by Reverend Parris, who had seen Tituba "waving her arms over the fire" and had heard "a screeching and gibberish coming from her mouth."

Upon seeing her father, Parris' daughter Betty fell into a kind of trance that doctors cannot explain medically. Although his niece Abigail vehemently denies it, Parris strongly suspects the girls are involved with witchcraft. He knows not only that witchcraft is punishable by death, but also that the consequences of such news getting out in the town are dire to his own reputation. For these reasons, he attempts to keep the rumors of witchcraft from spreading throughout the town. News from townspeople who come to speak with Parris suggests that it is already too late.

Ann and Thomas Putnam's daughter Ruth is in a trance similar to Betty's. Goody Putnam admits that she sent her daughter Ruth to Tituba to ask her to speak to the souls of her seven children who died in childbirth. She hoped to learn through this who had murdered her babies. Parris is horrified by this news. His voiced concern, however, is for himself rather than for the girls being involved with evil. Abigail and the Putnams convince him to go downstairs and address the crowd that has gathered, denouncing the devil.

While they are gone, Abigail confers with Mercy Lewis, the Putnam's servant who was also in the woods. Abigail attempts to put together a story they can tell the adults; however, another of the girls, Mary Warren, enters and argues for telling the truth. She is terrified of the punishment for witchcraft and would prefer to be whipped for merely dancing. Suddenly Betty begins to whimper and

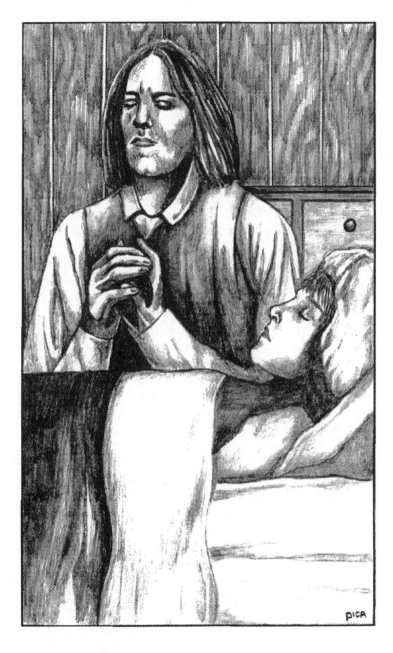

darts off the bed. She is convinced that she can fly to her mother, who has been dead for some time. Betty then reveals that Abigail drank blood in the woods as part of a charm to kill Elizabeth Proctor. This accusation infuriates Abigail, and she forcefully insists that the girls stick to the story that they were only dancing and that Tituba and Ruth alone conjured her dead sisters. She threatens great harm to anyone who breathes a word of the other things.

Analysis

In the written version of this play, Arthur Miller chose to add several narrative sections that were not included in the live performance. These sections give the reader a broader knowledge of characters' past actions and motivations. The opening narrative gives an introduction to Reverend Parris and his idiosyncrasies, which include a distorted view of other people's opinions of him and a driving need to be in control. These facts will go a long way toward explaining the minister's future behavior.

We also learn something about Salem's attitude toward children. Miller tells us that Paris, "like the rest of Salem, never conceived that the children were anything but thankful for being permitted to walk straight, eyes slightly lowered, arms at the sides, and mouths shut until bidden to speak." This is important because it leads us to believe that the children would welcome a respite from such a strict life, as well as a bit of attention from the adults of the town.

The third important point in the opening narrative is the fact that the people of Salem had a "predilection for minding other people's business." They believed very strongly that their way was the only right way, and they persecuted anyone who questioned their ideas. Because of this, it was very dangerous in Salem to be caught doing anything that could be construed as contrary to accepted behavior. The community saw, and could not explain, the sickness of the two girls, Betty and Ruth. Having a world view heavily weighted with devils and witches, it was perfectly reasonable in their minds to call anything unexplainable by earthly means the work of the devil.

The dramatic action of this opening sequence sets up many of the themes and conflicts central to the play. The defining metaphor of the play is a symbol that does not appear anywhere but in the title: the crucible. A crucible is a container used to heat metal to extremely high temperatures, refining it to its barest essence and melting away any foreign substances or impurities. A crucible is also defined as a "severe test or trial, especially one that causes a lasting change or influence." The events of the previous night will eventually test the entire community's moral fiber. The court will test those accused to see if their essence is essentially good or evil. The historic episode will test the character and belief system of everyone involved.

When the girls are discovered in the woods, they know that they will be judged, and judged harshly. The details of what actually happened build slowly as new characters add to the story. We know that the girls were dancing and that Parris believes he saw at least one girl dancing naked. We know that Tituba chanted over a cauldron of some type, and we later find out that she was attempting to conjure the souls of the Putnum's dead babies. We then discover that Abigail drank the blood of a chicken in an effort to put a curse on Elizabeth Proctor, her former employer. While to us these antics may seem harmless and rather silly, they added up to serious charges in Salem. The girls certainly knew the consequences, as is clear by their comments. Why then, would they engage in such behavior?

One theory is simple adolescent rebellion. The rules of such a strict society, with so little room for enjoyment, wore down their adolescent spirits until an outlet was sought. Tituba, with her relatively uninhibited island background, offered an opportunity for a freeing of their spirits. Another theory is that they were actually looking for attention. In a world in which children were typically ignored, they wanted to cause a ruckus that would briefly put them in the spotlight. Whatever the reason, two of the girls were so shocked at being discovered, and at the ultimate consequence of that discovery, that they immediately feigned illness. The failure of their illness to respond to medical attention is what begins all of the rumors of witchcraft.

It is interesting to note Parris' reaction to the situation. While his daughter lies gravely ill, beyond the help of medical science, and while rumors of demonic possession circulate through the

town, his thoughts are only for himself. Obviously if witchcraft is evil, witchcraft in the home of the minister—the pillar of the society and its moral leader—is doubly evil. Parris focuses all of his attention on saving his own reputation. To the citizens of Salem, a good reputation is an outward sign of rightness with God. This emphasis on a good name is a central theme of the play. The minister's first thought is to deny any element of witchcraft and hope the problem goes away. Unfortunately, Salem is a town full of people minding other people's business, and the gossip of witchcraft has already spread like wildfire. Many of the townspeople are already downstairs in the common room of Parris' house.

Parris suffers from a crucial lack of conviction. Although he is hesitant to call the events that have taken place witchcraft, he is easily convinced by the Putnams to go downstairs and denounce the evil in their midst. He is unable to tell his congregation that they are wrong about witchcraft. He prefers, instead, to do what he believes they want him to do. He goes along with the mounting hysteria and propels it forward by calling in Reverend Hale. This action paves the way for the absurdity that will follow.

The Putnams themselves set up a central conflict of the play, defining some of the suspicion, jealousy, and resentment simmering below the surface of this outwardly ordered and repressed society. When Ann Putnam admits to sending her daughter, Ruth, to conjure up the spirits of her dead babies, she reveals a strong suspicion and resentment. It occurs to her that there must be an explanation for seven of her children dying in childbirth, and she is looking for a scapegoat. She sent her daughter to get a name on which to attach blame. A narrative aside also tells us that Thomas Putnam still harbors resentment against those who voted against his brother-in-law as minister of Salem. The Putnams exemplify the feelings that must have existed throughout this society.

These feelings are echoed in the conflict between Abigail and Elizabeth Proctor, which is hinted at early in the play. When Parris questions Abigail's character, he mentions that she was dismissed as the Proctor's house servant. Rumor has obviously circulated in Salem that she was dismissed for unseemly behavior and that Elizabeth will not come to church and sit near "something soiled." Abigail's denial holds venomous words for her former employer, whom she calls "a bitter woman, a lying, cold, sniveling woman." Elizabeth had made her life unpleasant in several ways, and Abigail's attempt to put a curse on the woman by drinking chicken blood is a vivid manifestation of her feelings.

The exchange that takes place between the girls while the adults are gone is also telling. They argue amongst themselves between admitting the truth and denying everything. The sequence sets up the conflict between Abigail and Mary Warren, who argues for telling the truth. Mary is seen as weak and as the one who is most likely to tell on the others. The truth is obviously something less than dabbling in witchcraft, and to admit it and take the punishment would save them from being hanged as witches. Abigail, however, asserts herself as the strongest of the girls, bullying the others into admitting nothing other than the fact that they were dancing in the woods. This much is indisputable since they were caught in the act by Parris. Her intimidation of the others and the threats she makes should they disobey her orders show her unfeeling response to their fears. Abigail will have her way, whatever it takes to get it. This bit of evil in her character will be magnified as the play unfolds.

Study Questions

1. What do we learn in the opening narrative that is important to the events that follow?

2. What happened in the woods the night before Act One begins?

3. How did the events come to light, and what was the effect on Betty and Ruth?

4. Why is the town so stirred up by these events?

5. What is Reverend Parris' first reaction to the crisis?

6. What reason does Ann Putnam have to be resentful?

7. What reason does Thomas Putnam have to be resentful?

8. Why do the girls argue about whether or not to tell the truth?

9. How does Abigail eventually get her way?

10. What is a crucible?

Answers

1. We learn that Parris thinks everyone is out to get him and that he has a need to be in control. We also learn that the citizens of Salem mind each other's business and are unforgiving.

2. Several teenage girls of Salem were in the woods dancing, some of them naked. Tituba was trying to contact the dead, and Abigail was trying to put a curse on Elizabeth Proctor.

3. The girls were caught by Reverend Parris, and the shock caused Betty and Ruth to fall ill.

4. The town is stirred up because the girls cannot be healed, and they suspect witchcraft.

5. Parris' first reaction is to save his own name and reputation.

6. Ann Putnam suspects someone has been killing her babies in childbirth.

7. Thomas Putnam resents the fact that his candidate for minister of Salem was not elected.

8. To admit the truth means severe punishment for dancing and conjuring; to be found guilty of witchcraft means hanging.

9. Abigail forces the others not to tell the truth through intimidation and threats.

10. A crucible is a container in which metals are burned at high temperatures to burn off impurities; it is also defined as a severe test or trial.

Suggested Essay Topics

1. What does the opening narrative section add to the play? How would your judgment of what is happening on stage be different without this narrative section?

2. Examine the reasons the girls have for not telling the whole story of what happened in the woods. Base your discussion on the reactions of the main characters introduced so far and what you know of the society of Salem from the opening narrative.

Scene II: John Proctor's Entrance

New Characters:

John Proctor: *husband of Elizabeth, one of the few townspeople who try to stop the court*

Rebecca Nurse: *wife of Francis, accused of being a witch*

Giles Corey: *landowner of Salem who tries to save his wife, who is accused*

Summary

Mary and Mercy take their leave as John Proctor enters the stage. As he and Abigail speak alone, it becomes obvious that the two have had an affair. Abigail had been a housekeeper for the Proctors until John's wife, Elizabeth, became aware of the situation between the two and dismissed her. Abigail's attempts to revive the spark are rebuffed by Proctor, who has put the episode behind him. Abby tells Proctor that the rumors of witchcraft are ridiculous and that they were merely dancing in the woods. Meanwhile, as a psalm is sung in the room downstairs, Betty claps her hands over her ears and begins whining loudly. Parris and several others come rushing upstairs to see what has happened. Betty's behavior is taken as a sign of witchcraft, which has made it impossible for the girl to hear the Lord's name.

Next to enter are Rebecca Nurse and Giles Corey. A short narrative at this point gives a description of Rebecca's character, which is impeccable, and of the reasons why some of the townspeople might resent her. Rebecca's gentle presence calms Betty instantly; however, the adults are soon quarreling over the proper course of action. Rebecca and John Proctor provide the voice of reason, as the others call for an all-out witch-hunt. Both believe that the girls are just going through a short rebellious stage that they will soon outgrow. As they speak, it becomes clear that there is a division in the church's congregation between those who support Reverend

Parris and those who feel he is out of line. Angry words pass between Parris and Proctor about what the minister can expect from
the citizens of Salem. Shortly after, angry words are exchanged
between Proctor and Putnam, who accuses him of taking lumber
off land he does not own. Proctor and Corey are about to leave as
Reverend John Hale enters.

Analysis

The exchange between Abigail and John Proctor in this section sets up what is, perhaps, the central theme of the play. The
knowledge that the two have had an affair, and that Elizabeth discovered it and dismissed Abby, constitutes the conflict between
Abigail and Elizabeth. John clearly feels that what he did was wrong
and has tried to put the affair behind him. Abigail, however, wishes
their relationship would continue. She becomes the woman
scorned. Perhaps more importantly, Abby reveals the truth of the
events in the woods to John. She candidly admits to him that they
were merely dancing and that there was no witchcraft involved.
The possession of this truth, coupled with his guilt over his crime
of lechery with Abby, will later put John in the compromising position that ultimately leads to his death.

Some critics read *The Crucible* as the tragedy of John Proctor.
Proctor committed a tragic error and lost his soul when he had the
affair with Abby. The drama then becomes an attempt to find moral
absolution, integrity, and self-respect. Other critics have argued
with this interpretation on the grounds that Proctor is not a suffi-
cient tragic hero. He can succumb to temptation as well as stand
up for decency. Not a particularly good man, he is hardheaded,
argumentative, and biting in his criticism. He does not attend
church regularly. These characteristics, along with his thinly veiled
contempt of the minister, mark him as different from the rest of
the community. Proctor is a far more modern figure than any other
character in the play; skeptical and ruled by common sense rather
than accepted norms. Whether or not *The Crucible* is correctly
viewed as the tragedy of Proctor, a central theme of the play is certainly Proctor's search for his soul.

Betty's crying out at the Lord's name is just one more shred of
evidence for a community already convinced of witchcraft. Of

course her outburst also immediately followed John and Abby's discussion of their infidelity. Her adverse reaction could just as easily have stemmed from this newly gained knowledge, coupled with her remembrance of Abby's attempt to put a curse on Elizabeth. Betty Parris is already suffering from fear and guilt, and her desire to go to her mother is logical. The townspeople, however, are convinced that they are facing great evil, and everything that can possibly be twisted to lend credence to their conclusion will be used. Significantly, it is Rebecca Nurse who is instantly able to calm her.

Goody Nurse serves as a symbol of goodness and reason. Her character is impeccable, and her reputation flawless. Soon after her entrance, she dismisses the behavior of the girls as part of their "silly season" that they will soon outgrow. She sees the events of the night before as a natural outlet for adolescent emotions. Rebecca makes it quite clear that any searching for the devil in Salem based on the behavior of the girls is, in itself, an evil. Throughout the play, she and Proctor will represent the few consistent voices speaking reason and denouncing the proceedings as preposterous. In this scene Miller draws the conflict of Rebecca Nurse and John Proctor, two individual voices, against the voices of the rest of the society, a community caught up in the mass hysteria of the witch-hunt. Rebecca, however, is not as quick as Proctor to condemn the social order. While she agrees that there are problems with Salem's theocracy—and especially with its minister—she urges Proctor to keep peace with Parris.

Several other conflicts are set up in this scene as well. We learn that the Nurses have been involved in a land war with their neighbors, one of whom is Putnam The Nurse family was also among those who kept Putnam's candidate for minister out of office in Salem. Further, a group of people related to, or friendly with, the Nurses had broken away from the authority of Salem and set up their own independently governed town. The split was resented by many of the older members of the Salem community. The Nurses, in short, had many silent enemies in Salem. It is important to note that prior to the witch-hunt, there was no socially sanctioned means for expressing such ill will against a neighbor. The religious code required each citizen to love his neighbor as

himself. Any outward expression of hostility would have been se-
verely frowned upon. This led to a situation in which a great deal
of resentment was seething below the surface, with no outlet.

When the participants in this scene exchange angry words, it
is further apparent that the cause of the tension in Salem has very
little to do with witchcraft. Proctor's conflict with Parris stems from
what he sees to be the minister's hypocrisy of wanting more than
his due. Parris, in return, resents Proctor for arguing against his
having a higher salary. Nearly everyone else in town seems caught
up in the battle over land ownership, which represents status and
power in the community. The witch trials will become a convenient
forum in which to address these real or imagined wrongs.

Study Questions

1. Why was Abigail dismissed from her job at the Proctor's house?
2. What does Abby tell Proctor about the events in the woods?
3. How have Proctor's feelings toward Abby changed?
4. When does Betty cry out?
5. How is this cry interpreted?
6. How is Betty finally calmed?
7. How does Rebecca explain the events in the woods?
8. Why would anyone resent the Nurses?
9. Why does Proctor dislike Parris?
10. Why does Parris dislike Proctor?

Answers

1. Abigail was dismissed from her job when Elizabeth discovered her affair with John.
2. Abby tells Proctor that they were merely dancing and that there was no witchcraft involved.
3. Proctor has put the affair behind him and no longer welcomes Abby's advances.

4. Betty cries out when she hears the name of the Lord sung downstairs.

5. The cry is interpreted as another sign of witchcraft. If Betty is possessed by a demonic spirit, she cannot bear to hear the name of the Lord.

6. Rebecca Nurse seems to calm Betty merely by her presence.

7. Rebecca feels the events in the woods were merely expressions of adolescent foolishness.

8. The Nurses have been involved in a land war with their neighbors and were among those who kept Putnam's candidate for minister out of office in Salem.

9. Proctor despises what he sees as Parris' outrageous hypocrisy and greed.

10. Parris resents Proctor for arguing against paying him more money.

Suggested Essay Topics

1. How are Rebecca Nurse and John Proctor different from the other characters in this sequence? How do they compare and contrast to each other?

2. Why does Betty's behavior appear to be witchcraft? How else might it be explained?

Scene III: John Hale's Entrance

New Character:

Reverend John Hale: *minister from Boston, who is summoned to determine if there is witchcraft in Salem*

Summary

A short narrative section discusses Reverend Hale's arrival and some theology involving the devil. Hale then listens to an account of the events that have taken place and consults the large books about witchcraft that he has brought with him. Rebecca makes it clear that she strongly disapproves of this effort to seek the devil, and exits. Giles, however, is caught up in the appearance of greatness. He asks Hale why his wife reads strange books and why the reading of them seems to stop his prayers. Another narrative points out that Giles has only recently learned any prayers and that he is a crank and a nuisance in the town. Hale promises to look into the matter.

Hale presses Abigail for details of the night's events. Abigail admits that there was a frog in the cauldron that Tituba tended and that Tituba called the devil. Tituba is summoned, and Abigail immediately points to her and accuses, "She made me do it. She made Betty do it." Then Abigail accuses Tituba of making her drink chicken blood. Tituba denies involvement with the devil, but Abigail persists in her accusations. Soon she is saying that Tituba sends her spirit on her in church and makes her laugh during prayer and that she comes to her at night and makes her drink blood and remove her clothes.

Tituba is terrified and tells Hale that the devil has many witches and it must be someone else that is affecting the children. The two ministers press her to identify townspeople who were with the devil. Tituba, in her fear, is pushed to name Sarah Good and Goody Osburn. After seeing all the praise and encouragement given to Tituba, Abigail joins in as well. She says she saw Sarah Good, Goody

Osburn, and Bridget Bishop with the devil. Then Betty rises from her bed and joins the chant. The curtain falls on the two young girls calling out name after name, as the ministers praise God for this revelation of evil in their midst.

Analysis

The introductory narrative section at Hale's entrance helps us understand his motivation. Hale has studied the matter of witchcraft intensively and is regarded as an expert on the spirit world. We know that Hale is proud of his position as the authority on witches and that he will zealously seek an opportunity to make use of his knowledge. Miller tells us that there was once an encounter with a suspected witch in Hale's parish; however, on closer examination, it turned out that the woman was not a witch at all. It was simply her annoying behavior that caused a child to act "afflicted." Hale never has then encountered a substantiated case of witchcraft. Hale's previous experience, as well as his intellectual nature, should lead him first to look for a natural and logical explanation for the behavior of the Salem girls. Instead, he begins with the supernatural, trying to fit the events he finds before him into his definition of deviltry.

Miller explains in this narrative passage the history of diabolism and the world's long history of fear and hatred of opposites. A natural outgrowth of this is aligning one's enemies with the devil. In a world in which actions and ideas are attributable either to God or to Satan, he says, the devil can be used as a weapon. This particular phrasing foreshadows the development of the witch-hunt, where many people will be accused for personal gain or satisfaction. Witchcraft is not an act that can be documented, such as stealing or murder. Its evidence is by nature circumstantial, and it therefore lends itself to such misuse.

The timing of Hale's entrance is significant. He arrives immediately after the heated discussion that revealed the many conflicts among town residents. Hale is an outsider in Salem. He knows nothing of the land wars, the behavior of the minister, or the numerous secret animosities harbored by the townspeople. The discussion prior to his entrance would have supplied him with ample reason to suspect explanations other than witchcraft. Hale appears to be a likable man—well respected and trying his best to lend his assistance to a troubled community. Miller compares him to a doctor on his first call, armed with his knowledge and eager to use it. He attempts, however, to apply the authority of his books, along with the authority of scripture, to a situation about which he knows frightfully little. He is like a doctor who has no knowledge of the greatest and most telling symptom.

The introductions made when Hale arrives are also important. From them we learn that Rebecca Nurse's good name is known well beyond the town limits of Salem. Hale's knowledge of her good character is what will later lead him to question his involvement in the trial proceedings. As John Proctor is introduced to Hale, Giles Corey tells the visitor that he does not believe in witches. Proctor has been set up as the skeptic; the individual who refuses to be involved with what he believes to be unreasonable behavior. Although Proctor shrugs off the remark and takes no position, the thought has been planted in Hale's mind. It will later be used against Proctor when is wife is accused.

Both Proctor and Rebecca remove themselves from the proceedings before the actual questioning begins. Both have made it clear that they believe talk of witchcraft is nonsense. Rebecca has also implied that it is the actual searching for the devil that is evil. Proctor knows from his discussion with Abigail that there was nothing supernatural occurring in the woods. Both choose to alienate themselves from the struggle that consumes the rest of Salem. This decision will later prove to be costly. Miller explores here the issue of an individual's responsibility to the community in crisis. Merely by keeping themselves removed from the hysteria, these two characters bring suspicion upon themselves. They are a threat to the unity of the community.

When Hale begins to question Betty, Abigail, and Tituba, it is clear that he knows what he is looking for. The girls do not offer information; it is suggested to them. As soon as Abby becomes uncomfortable with the questioning, she attempts to remove the blame from herself and pin it on Tituba. Suddenly she admits all of her "anti-Puritan" behavior, but claims that it was Tituba who forced her to act. Tituba is a natural choice for a scapegoat. She is exotic in Salem, a native of Barbados where strange and

incomprehensible customs are practiced. She is a far more believable "witch" than any of the others.

Tituba is understandably terrified at the accusations. While at
first she denies all connection with the devil, she soon sees that
her only way out is to come up with another explanation. She tells
the interrogators that the devil has many witches. While Tituba has
denied involvement with the devil, Hale is so sure of what he will
find that he begins to question her about it anyway. Tituba can
endure such bullying and confusion for only so long. The men are
so kind to her when she finally says that there are women in Salem
who are witches that she suddenly begins to cooperate with them,
inventing conversations with the devil and indicating the name Sarah Good. Abigail sees the enthusiasm with which Tituba's
accusations are received and decides to try the tactic herself. She,
too, begins to name names. Finally, Betty also rises and joins in.
The three women have discovered a way out of their predicament.
Far from being punished for their behavior, they are now heroes of
the community, chosen to help cleanse Salem. The naming of
names is taken as an outward sign of their repentance and desire
to be better Christians.

It is important to realize that while the girls are confessing to
things that were not done, they are, indeed, guilty of something.
While they were not performing witchcraft, they were involved with
actions that were serious sins in the Puritan tradition. Dancing
alone would bring serious punishment. The witch-hunt does not
create guilt, it merely unleashes what is already there. The girls are
attempting to hide their very real guilt by complying with the witch-
hunt. The theme of guilt is strong throughout the play and will be
even more important in the actions of John Proctor.

Study Questions

1. Why is Hale invited to Salem from Boston?

2. Has Hale ever found a witch?

3. What is significant about the timing of Hale's entrance?

4. What do we learn about Rebecca Nurse from Hale?

5. What does Giles mention to Hale about Proctor?

6. What does Giles mention about his wife?

7. What are Rebecca and John's roles in the proceedings?

8. What does Abigail do when questioned?

9. How is Tituba treated when she finally concocts a conversation with the devil and names a Salem woman as a witch?

10. What does Abby do when she sees this reaction?

Answers

1. Hale is a noted authority on witchcraft.

2. Hale once thought he had found a witch, but thorough investigation revealed that there was a natural explanation for the questionable behavior.

3. Hale enters immediately after the conversation that reveals the conflicts among the residents of Salem.

4. We learn that Rebecca's good reputation is widely known.

5. Giles tells Hale that Proctor does not believe in witches.

6. Giles tells Hale that his wife reads books and that when she is reading them, he cannot pray.

7. Both Rebecca and John refuse to be involved in the witch-hunt.

8. Abigail pins the blame on Tituba.

9. Tituba is greatly encouraged and treated like a hero.

10. Abby seeks the same kind of attention and begins naming names herself.

Suggested Essay Topics

1. Explore the various ways Abby explains her behavior in the woods to different characters in the play. What are the motives for each of her explanations?

2. Discuss John Proctor as an individual at odds with authority and with his community.

Act II

Scene I: John and Elizabeth Proctor

New Character:

Elizabeth Proctor: *wife of John Proctor, accused of witchcraft*

Summary

Act Two is set in John Proctor's house, in the common room downstairs, several days after the events of Act One. As the curtain opens, Elizabeth is heard singing to the children upstairs. John enters, tastes the soup in the pot over the fireplace, and re-seasons it. Elizabeth comes downstairs and the two sit down to dinner, making small talk about the crops. It is apparent that there is a tension between them. Elizabeth informs John that their house-keeper, Mary Warren, is now an official of the newly-formed court in Salem. Four judges have been sent from Boston, headed by Deputy Governor Danforth. Fourteen people have been jailed for witchcraft, and the court has the power to hang them if they do not confess.

Elizabeth attempts to persuade John to go to Salem and tell the court that the witchcraft accusations are a fraud. After all,

Abigail herself, who is now chief of the accusers, told John that the matter had nothing to do with witchcraft. John, however, hesitates to go. He is not sure that he can prove what Abigail said to him. There are no witnesses; the two were alone. On learning that John was alone with Abby, Elizabeth is deeply hurt and an argument is sparked between them over his involvement with the girl.

Analysis

John's simple act of re-seasoning the soup is symbolic of the nature of the relationship between John and Elizabeth. As the soup has little flavor, so does their marriage. While Elizabeth is quiet and virtuous, she has none of the individual spirit associated with her husband. She appears to be, and has been accused by Abigail of being, a cold woman. She "receives" John's kiss, rather than returning it, and she fails to enliven the house with flowers. It is not hard to imagine that John could be attracted to the daring, individualist spirit of Abigail and her raw sexuality. Elizabeth is a sharp contrast to such a girl.

The tension between John and Elizabeth is thick as they sit down to dinner. While unfailingly polite, their relationship is visibly strained. John's previous indiscretions with Abby have not yet been forgiven, despite his attempts to make amends. John has clearly tried to put the issue in his past. He has shown in Parris' house that he will no longer entertain thoughts of a relationship with Abby. Elizabeth, however, continues to interrogate and to accuse. Her judgment of her husband lacks mercy and understanding. This lack of mercy will be mirrored later in the play in the proceedings of the court.

The issue of guilt is strong in this sequence. John is clearly guilty of his infidelity. However willing he may be to repent, his position offers him no opportunity for absolution. He is not denying that he has sinned. He has clearly violated his own sense of honor by behaving as he did. John has suffered greatly for his sin, both internally and externally in Elizabeth's reaction. He has already questioned his identity in light of his actions. Elizabeth's harsh judgment of him makes his search for his soul and his "name"

throughout the play all the more difficult. She stubbornly insists on the reality of his guilt. This atmosphere of guilt will later be obvious to Hale and lead to dire consequences.

Through Elizabeth we learn how far the girls' "confessions" have gone. A court system has been newly established in Salem, headed by Deputy Governor Danforth. It is significant that such a court has not existed before in Salem. Up to this point, the social fabric of the community was so tightly woven that an official court was unnecessary. Anything not sanctioned by scripture was, without question, a violation of the moral code, and punishments were set and accepted. The witch-hunt, however, goes far beyond any accusation seen in Salem up to that point. Because the evidence is circumstantial, a court must be established to weigh the evidence and attempt to make fair and honest judgments. Elizabeth knows that the foundation of the court itself is not genuine.

In trying to convince John to go to the court and convince the others that the trials are a fraud, Elizabeth is imposing a sense of duty on her husband. John has no patience for authority of any sort, and he strongly resents Elizabeth telling him what to do. He is caught in the dilemma of knowing the truth and being unwilling to tell it. Abby's confession was offered to him alone. There were no witnesses. He knows that it will be his word against Abby's. John knows what Abby is capable of, and he fears for his name. Should the knowledge of his affair with Abigail become public, his reputation in Salem will be destroyed. John is beginning to discover that he cannot escape the implications of his past actions. He struggles with these issues, as well as with his desire to remain uninvolved.

The conflict between Mary Warren and the Proctors is also established in this sequence. While the girl has not yet entered the house, Elizabeth describes how her meek and timid manner has changed. Mary's association with the court has given her power and attention she has not previously known. She has become openly defiant of her employers' orders and has neglected her duties at the house. This change in Mary, alluded to here, will be developed in the next sequence.

Study Questions

1. What is the significance of John's re-seasoning the soup?

2. What is the relationship between John and Elizabeth like?

3. What new position does Mary Warren now hold?

4. Who is in charge of this court?

5. What action has the court taken?

6. What will happen if the accused do not confess?

7. How has Mary's personality changed since her involvement in the court?

8. What issue does Elizabeth continue to hound her husband about?

9. What does Elizabeth's lack of mercy and understanding fore-shadow?

10. Why does John hesitate to go to the court and reveal Abigail's fraud?

Answers

1. The unseasoned soup is a symbol of the Proctors' flavorless marriage.

2. The relationship between John and Elizabeth is tense and strained.

3. Mary is now an official in the newly formed court.

4. The court consists of four judges sent from Boston.

5. The court has accused 14 Salemites of witchcraft.

6. If the accused do not confess, they will be hanged.

7. Mary used to be timid and shy, but is now openly defiant of her employer.

8. Elizabeth cannot forgive John's indiscretion with Abigail.

9. Elizabeth's behavior towards John foreshadows the later actions of the court.

10. John hesitates because he does not like to be ordered by Elizabeth and because he fears he will not be believed, since there are no other witnesses to Abby's confession.

Suggested Essay Topics

1. Compare the character of Elizabeth Proctor to that of Mary Warren. What value systems do each represent?

2. Discuss Elizabeth's reaction to John's infidelity. Is she being unreasonable?

Scene II: Mary Warren's Entrance

Summary

As John and Elizabeth wrangle over John's guilt, Mary Warren enters. John grabs her immediately, furious that she should shirk her duties and go to Salem without his permission. Mary responds by offering Elizabeth a doll that she sewed for her during the trials that day. Elizabeth is puzzled by the gift, but accepts it. Mary then reveals that there are now 39 arrested, and that Goody Osburn will be hanged. Sarah Good, however, confessed to making a pact with the devil and will not hang. Mary also reveals that Sarah is pregnant, and the court will surely spare her to save her unborn child.

Mary then tells John and Elizabeth that she must go to Salem every day to sit on the court. John forbids her and takes out the whip to give her a beating. She saves herself, however, by revealing that Elizabeth herself was accused that day but was saved by Mary's testimony that she had never seen any signs of witchcraft in the house. Mary uses this bit of power to assert herself before a disgusted John Proctor. Mary then goes to bed.

Elizabeth and John are shocked by the news. Elizabeth knows that Abigail is jealous that she has John and that this is a perfect opportunity to pry Elizabeth from her husband. She asks John to talk to Abby and break the unspoken spell between them. John grudgingly agrees to go.

Analysis

The rapid escalation of hysteria in Salem is subtly revealed here in the news from Mary Warren. Where the girl reported 14 were arrested the previous day, the total now stands at 39. The mere quantity of citizens involved should surely have alerted someone to the absurdity of the charges. The evidence against the "witches" is unreasonable enough to be ridiculous. Even actions such as mumbling have been interpreted as witchcraft. At this point, however, the court has already extracted a confession from Sarah Good.

Put in the untenable position of confessing to witchcraft and being warmly welcomed back into the community or not confessing and hanging for it, Goody Good chose to save her life. The effect of her confession will have broad-reaching consequences for the others. Had she not confessed, it would have been far more difficult for the court to hang anyone. Now that the court has at least one confession, the guilt of the others is far more sure in the court's eyes. With Sarah's confession, the court has reached a point of no return.

The gift of the poppet is significant. Elizabeth is perplexed by the gift, as she is a grown woman. Puritan society was not given to frivolousness. In a community where even children were expected to act like adults, such an item would not be expected to grace a woman's home. It will later be quite significant that Mary Warren brought the doll into the house. Mary's strange declaration that "We must all love each other now" as she hands the gift to Elizabeth is in strong contrast to the intensified conflict between the girl and the Proctors shortly thereafter. Not only is Mary defiant to Elizabeth, she now stands up to John as well. John's temper is apparent as he attempts to beat her for her arrogance.

As disturbing as this news of the courts is to the Proctors, the truly shocking revelation is yet to come. Mary reveals that Elizabeth herself had been named as a possible witch that day. The girl escapes a beating by telling her employers that she put in a good word for Elizabeth, telling them that she told the court she never witnessed any witchcraft in the house. Elizabeth immediately recognizes the accusation against her as a plot by Abigail to remove her from John's side. The animosity between the two women has now become dangerous. Abigail is the chief accuser of the court and is now calling the shots. Whatever she says is being taken as gospel, however bizarre. She is in a position to take revenge on Elizabeth for dismissing her and on John for ending their affair. Elizabeth sees that Abigail is still under John's spell, and she begs her husband to break it.

Proctor was already reluctant to approach the court and reveal the fraud. Despite the danger to Elizabeth, he remains unwilling to do so. At this point John is still able to believe in the ultimate justice of the court. Sure that her innocence will be easily proven, he hesitates to take orders from his wife. While he does ultimately decide to go, it is not by his own choice, but through pressure from Elizabeth. He stubbornly maintains his individuality and refusal to be involved until he is nagged into doing otherwise. John despises the court and all it stands for, but his family has been dragged into the crisis despite all his attempts to remain aloof. His failure to respond to the crisis represents an abnegation of his personal responsibility.

Study Questions

1. What does Mary Warren give Elizabeth?
2. What is Elizabeth's reaction to the gift?
3. How many people have now been arrested?
4. What will happen to those who do not confess?
5. Who has confessed?
6. What does this mean for the others?
7. What would spare Sarah Good from hanging?
8. What shocking news does Mary offer regarding Elizabeth?
9. What cause does Elizabeth immediately suspect?
10. Now that Elizabeth is accused, does John go quickly to the court to clear her name?

Answers

1. Mary gives Elizabeth a poppet, or doll, that she had sewn that day in court.
2. Elizabeth is surprised. A doll is an odd gift to give a grown woman.
3. A total of 39 people have now been arrested.
4. Those who do not confess will be hanged.
5. Sarah Good has confessed.
6. Now that one person has confessed, the charges against the others are more believable.

7. Sarah is pregnant, and the court will spare her unborn child.

8. Mary reveals that Elizabeth has been accused of witchcraft.

9. Elizabeth suspects the accusation was an attempt by Abigail to eventually marry John.

10. Even though Elizabeth has been accused, John hesitates to go to the court. He agrees to go only after being coerced by his wife.

Suggested Essay Topics

1. Discuss how Mary Warren's character has changed from Act One to Act Two. What are the causes of these changes?

2. Discuss the various "evidences" of witchcraft used to convict the witches. Why do these particular charges hold any weight?

Scene III: John Hale's Visit

New Character:

Francis Nurse: *husband of Rebecca Nurse*

Summary

Reverend Hale appears at the door as John is about to leave to talk to Abby. He tells the Proctors that Elizabeth's name has been mentioned in the court. His mission is to determine the Christian character of the Proctors. Hale is concerned that John does not attend every Sunday and asks him for a reason. At first John offers the reason that Elizabeth had been sick. Soon, however, he cannot keep from telling Hale of his differences with Reverend Parris, who is always looking for more money. When Hale asks why one of his sons is not baptized, John tells him that he does not want the minister's hand on his baby. He "does not see the light of God" in Parris.

Hale is still a bit unsure of the Proctor's religion. He asks them to repeat their commandments. John nervously gets through nine, but cannot think of the tenth. Elizabeth gently indicates that he has left out adultery. John is uneasy, and Hale is obviously concerned by this lapse. As Hale is about to leave, obviously unconvinced of Elizabeth's innocence, she suddenly begs John to tell Hale what Abby told him. John haltingly tells Hale that the sickness of the children has nothing to do with witchcraft. He suggests that those who have confessed may have done so only to save themselves from hanging. This suggestion strikes a cord with Hale, who has obviously entertained the thought himself. He then questions the Proctors on their belief in witches. When Elizabeth asserts that she cannot believe in witches, Hale is shocked.

Giles Corey and Francis Nurse then arrive with the news that both of their wives have been taken to jail. Martha Corey's charge is bewitching a farmer so that he cannot keep pigs alive; Rebecca's is murdering Goody Putnam's babies. While Hale was able to doubt Elizabeth, whom he did not know, he is truly shaken by the news

that Rebecca Nurse has been charged. Her good character and deeds of charity were known far from Salem; however, he asserts his faith in the court and his belief that Rebecca's innocence will be proved.

Analysis

The issue of John's not attending church regularly is larger than it might seem. Not only is it expected of a good Christian, it also represents a sense of community. His failure to attend church regularly is an outward manifestation of his dangerous nonconformity that threatens the foundation of the society. John is openly hostile to Salem's obsession with sin. For that he will be punished.

The matter of not baptizing one of his sons is a far more serious offense. To the Puritans, a baby would not enter heaven if it had not been baptized and thus accepted as a child of God. Whether or not John believes this, his failure to baptize his son indicates the depth of his negative feelings toward the minister. This act in itself would surely bring the community to question his reputation. Proctor's open criticism of the materialism of the minister is a challenge to the minister's authority.

Hale's questioning of the Proctors is another example of the string of interrogations in Act Two that began with Elizabeth's interrogation of her husband. When John reveals his conflict with the minister, Hale should begin to see underlying causes for the accusations of witchcraft. Instead, he allows his ideology to hide the evidence presented to his reason. John's explanations for his failure to attend services and to baptize his son are reasonable and complete. There is no reason his faith should be tested further.

Hale, however, persists in pressing the Proctors. When asked to repeat the commandments, John noticeably forgets adultery. This "Freudian slip" shows that John has not yet come to terms with his guilt over the affair with Abigail. John's visible discomfort is due to his overwhelming sense of his own sin. Elizabeth has created an atmosphere of guilt that could be felt by Hale. His suspicion aroused, he presses for details, knowing the commandments were a frequent sign of faith. It is often offered as a defense of character, and in Sarah Good's case, her failure to repeat them eventually led to her conviction as a witch. John's hesitation is taken as a significant sign by Hale.

Giles Corey's offhanded comment about John's belief in witches now surfaces as another accusation against him. Hale is, after all, the authority on witches. He takes them very seriously. Elizabeth's assertion that she cannot believe if she herself is accused of being one is a significant breach of Christian behavior. It shows an alienation from the community more typical of John than of herself.

The first realization that something is amiss in the witch-hunt proceedings comes to Hale when he learns that Rebecca Nurse has now been accused. As an outsider, he is unfamiliar with nearly everyone in Salem. Rebecca, however, has a reputation for devoutness and charity that has reached him in Boston. Surely such a woman could not be a witch! While this bit of news does shake Hale, it is not enough to convince him that the court is a fraud. As he had said earlier, the most pious members of the community are far more valuable and challenging targets for the devil. He points out that Lucifer himself was as beautiful as any other angel before he fell. Hale still has faith that the truth will win out, and Rebecca will be released if she is innocent. The incident is important, though, in that up to this point Hale has refused to admit any thought that the trials may not be just.

Study Questions

1. Why does Hale appear at the Proctor house?

2. Why would John's Christian character be in question?

3. What reason does John first give for not going to church regularly?

4. What reason does John finally admit to for his behavior?

5. Why is John's not going to church significant to the play?

6. What does Hale request the Proctors do to show their faith?

7. Are the Proctors successful in fulfilling this request?

8. Why is this particular commandment significant?

9. What news briefly shakes Hale's belief in the court system?

10. What is his ultimate conclusion about the system at the end of this scene?

Answers

1. Hale travels to the Proctor house to question them on their Christian character.

2. John's faith is in question because he does not attend church regularly and has not had his third son baptized.

3. John explains that Elizabeth has been sick and he has stayed home to care for her.

4. John admits his animosity toward Reverend Parris.

5. It shows his failure to conform to the rules of the society and to participate in the community.

6. The Proctors are asked to repeat the commandments.

7. John can name nine commandments but forgets the commandment against adultery.

8. John's adultery with Abigail makes this particular commandment significant.

9. Hale's belief in the system is briefly shaken by the accusation of Rebecca Nurse.

10. Hale still believes that the innocent will be pardoned and justice will prevail.

Suggested Essay Topics

1. What signs does Hale look for in testing the Proctors' Christian character? What does it mean to be a good Puritan?

2. What information has been revealed to Hale at this point that should lead him to question the witch hunt? What keeps him from seeing it?

Scene IV: Cheever and Herrick's Entrance

New Characters:

Ezekiel Cheever: *clerk of the court, responsible for serving warrants to the accused*

Marshal Herrick: *an officer of the court, charged with chaining the accused to bring them to the prison*

Summary

Shortly after the disturbing news that Goody Nurse and Goody Corey have been charged, Ezekiel Cheever and Marshal Herrick enter the room. Cheever bears a warrant for Elizabeth's arrest and has been ordered to search the house for poppets. The two men are uncomfortable with their position and a bit afraid of John Proctor. Cheever spots the poppet that Mary made for Elizabeth that day in court. Upon examining the doll, a long needle is found stuck in its stomach. A horrified Cheever explains to the others that Abigail Williams had collapsed screaming at dinner, a needle stuck into her belly. When asked how she had been stabbed, Abby testified that it was Elizabeth's spirit. Mary is summoned to explain how the poppet came to be in the house and admits that she probably left the needle there herself. Her assertion, however, does not convince the others. John is so enraged at their behavior that he tears up the warrant and orders them to leave, asserting that it is not witchcraft that has taken hold of Salem, but vengeance.

All of John's anger, however, cannot prevent the men from taking Elizabeth away. Neither can he prevent them from chaining her for the journey. After the others leave, Proctor orders Mary to come with him to the court the next day and tell the truth about the poppet and how the needle came to be stuck in it. He cannot bear for Elizabeth to suffer for his own indiscretion. Mary, however, warns Proctor that if she goes against Abby, Abby will charge him with lechery and ruin him. The terrified girl is afraid that if

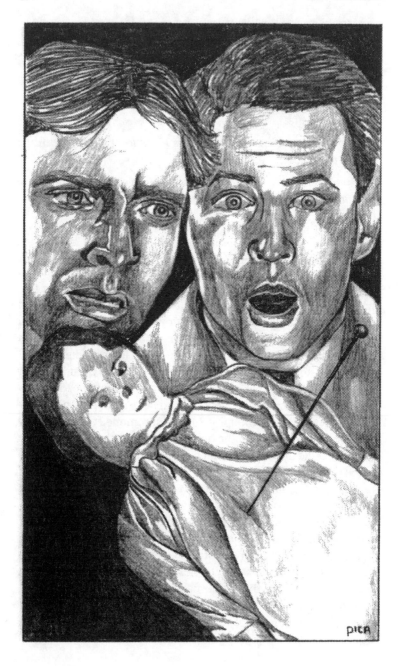

she tells the truth, the others will turn on her. She insists until the curtain closes that she cannot.

Analysis

The poppet represents the lengths to which Abigail is willing to go to seek vengeance. It is now clear that the doll was planted in the house by Mary Warren. Abigail has stuck her own belly with a long needle. She was simulating the voodoo practice of sewing a doll in someone's likeness, which is then used to inflict pain on that person. Abigail knows that there is no evidence of witchcraft in the Proctor household. The only way to implicate Elizabeth is to manufacture evidence. The hysteria in Salem has reached such a fevered pitch that even Mary's admission that she left the needle in the doll herself will not clear Elizabeth's name. At this point Abby is deliberately giving false evidence for her own personal gratification. She need not have legitimate proof. The court will believe only what it desires to believe. Their fanaticism has overcome their common sense and has created a new, subjective reality.

Cheever and Herrick represent the kind of blind loyalty to the social order that Proctor so despises. While they are decent men and have known the people they are arresting for years, they are bound by the law to take them unquestioningly. It is precisely this handing over of conscience to the state that Proctor strives to avoid. Cheever and Herrick have lost their sense of individual identity. They find it easier to conform than to think about their actions.

Proctor vividly shows his abhorrence of the court by tearing up the warrant for Elizabeth's arrest. He has correctly identified the cause of the hysteria as vengeance rather than justice, and he refuses to comply. Proctor believes that he is not bound to obey an unjust law. Why, he asks, has no one thought to question whether Parris or Abigail are being honest? Now, he says, "the little crazy children are jangling the keys of the kingdom, and common vengeance writes the law!" The accusers are always right, no matter how absurd the charge.

Proctor is still trying desperately to remain uninvolved in the witch-hunt procedures. When Elizabeth is taken away, however, he realizes that he can no longer remain on the sidelines. His wife's arrest has shown him the goodness of her character. He must do

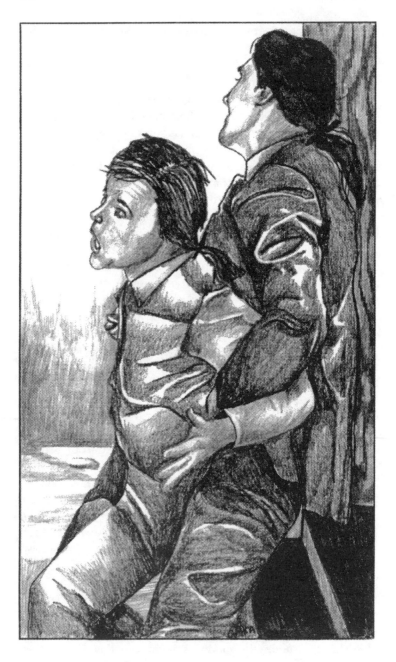

anything he can to clear her name. Still believing, however, that his own testimony will not convince the court, he enlists a terrified Mary Warren to tell her story. Mary gives him the ominous warning that should he attempt to interfere, Abigail will charge him with lechery and destroy his name. Proctor is being blackmailed. Once Proctor has made up his mind to stand up for his principles, however, this will not stop him.

Study Questions

1. What orders do Cheever and Herrick have at the Proctor house?

2. What has happened to Abigail?

3. Why is this related to the poppet?

4. Did Elizabeth keep poppets in her house?

5. What is found in the poppet?

6. How did the needle get there?

7. Do the authorities believe Mary's admission?

8. What does John do with the warrant for Elizabeth's arrest?

9. What does Proctor believe is motivating the court at this point?

10. What does Mary warn will happen if Proctor attempts to interfere with the court?

Answers

1. Cheever and Herrick are to search the Proctor's house for poppets and to arrest Elizabeth.

2. Abigail's belly has been pierced deeply with a long needle.

3. The poppet was found with a needle sticking out of its belly. It was commonly believed that dolls were kept by witches and manipulated in order to torture people.

4. Elizabeth never had poppets in the house until that day, when Mary gave her one.

5. A long needle is found in the poppet in the same place Abigail had been stabbed.

6. Mary Warren admits that she may have left it there when she made it.

7. The authorities pay no attention to Mary's admission.

8. John tears up the warrant for Elizabeth's arrest.

9. Proctor believes the court is now motivated entirely by vengeance.

10. Mary tells Proctor that Abigail will accuse him of lechery if he attempts to interfere.

Suggested Essay Topics

1. What is it that finally motivates Proctor to get involved?

2. How are the "little crazy children jangling the keys of the kingdom"?

Act III

Scene I: Charges of Fraud

New Characters:

Judge Hathorne: *one of the judges in the witch trials*

Deputy Governor Danforth: *the chief judge of the witch trials*

Summary

Act Three is set in the side room of the Salem meeting house, which has now become the General Court. The proceedings of the court, taking place in the next room, are audible. Judge Hathorne questions Martha Corey, who has been accused of reading fortunes and harming the accusing children. She denies the charges, and her husband Giles speaks out that he has evidence to present, accusing Thomas Putnam of attempting to acquire more land.

Giles is promptly thrown physically out of the courtroom and into the side room by Herrick. Hale soon follows, and then Judge Hathorne, Deputy Governor Danforth, Ezekiel Cheever, Francis Nurse, and Reverend Parris. Giles is soundly rebuffed for his disruption of the court proceedings, yet persists in claiming his wife's

innocence. He feels enormous guilt for mentioning Martha's fascination with books and thereby possibly bringing this trouble upon her.

Francis Nurse then shocks the judges by asserting that the girls are a fraud. He is promptly denounced as being in contempt of court. John Proctor escorts Mary Warren into the room to speak to Danforth and to hand him her signed deposition saying she saw no spirits. Danforth, however, refuses to accept any depositions. Mary openly admits that the behavior of all the girls is mere pretense. This admission calls into question the very foundation of the court, and Danforth suspects that this group is trying to undermine the court and, by extension, his authority.

Analysis

The stage directions to Act Three indicate that sunlight streams into the room from two high windows in the back wall. Similarly, the lighting in Act Four will be moonlight seeping through the bars of a high window. Miller's use of lighting adds another dimension to the symbolism of the novel. In an atmosphere of darkness, ignorance, and evil, a few shafts of pure light are visible coming from above, symbolizing goodness and truth. Unfortunately, while the light burns brightly, it is not enough to overcome the overwhelming darkness of the witch-hunts.

The subjective reality created in Salem is so strong at this point that the leaders feel no need to prove themselves to the world of reason and experience. Miller states in Act One that these were a people who felt "that they held in their steady hands the candle that would light the world." The Puritans clung to principles, and they attempted to live and die by them. This system of moral absolutes and life values is not, however, corrupt in itself. Characters like Rebecca Nurse and John Proctor value both reason and religion and lead a balanced life. It is the perversion of these values that becomes dangerous and even evil; the rejection of reality in favor of a system. The false accusation of witches where no witches exist is a mockery of the spiritual values the Puritans upheld. The play's strong emphasis on truth, as seen in the characters of Rebecca and the Proctors, shows a sympathy for the Puritan beliefs, rightly and reasonably applied.

The character of Danforth embodies the wrongful application of these values. Like Hale, Danforth is an outsider in Salem. While Hale at least attempted to investigate those accused, Danforth has no interest in the defendants as people. He measures his worth by the number of people he has jailed and sentenced to death. The Salem trials will bring him recognition and further his position as a judge. These selfish motives are mixed with a strong desire to maintain the status quo. Danforth is so strongly committed to maintaining the order created by the belief system that the ends justify the means. Political authority and religious authority are one and the same in Salem, and Danforth upholds what he strongly believes is the unarguable truth.

The precariousness of goodness in this world is underlined by the court's actions in Act Three. When Giles Corey attempts to offer a reasonable explanation for the accusations of the girls, he is removed from the court. Clearly the proceedings are taking place in a realm far beyond reason. Corey has put his finger on the truth. Putnam has been having his daughter name names of those whose land he wishes to obtain. According to the laws of Salem, a convicted witch must forfeit his or her land. Anyone with enough capital is then given the opportunity to buy it. Corey's accusation offers a convincing, though cold-blooded, motive; a rational explanation to replace the supernatural one. The court, though, is unwilling to consider that it may be mistaken.

The second attempt to sway the judges is offered by Francis Nurse, who openly accuses Danforth of being deceived. Judge Hathorne would have both Corey and Nurse arrested for contempt of court. Any evidence that conflicts with the girls will not be heard. It becomes clear that only the girls themselves can save the victims of this madness. When Mary Warren arrives and denounces the proceedings as mere pretense, she undermines the very foundation of the court system. Rather than believe the girl, the entire group is charged with attempting to overthrow the power of the court, which is entirely based on the contention that "the voice of Heaven is speaking through the children."

The significance of Mary's arrival is not lost on Parris. His position at the center of the proceedings is in jeopardy and he is not pleased. He attempts to undermine the effect of any testimony by

warning the judges that Proctor is "mischief." The trials have become a means for Parris to solidify his shaky position in Salem.
Where at first he was only a commentator, in Act Three he takes on
the role of accuser, making sure no possible charge is missed. While
issues such as church attendance and plowing on Sunday have no
bearing whatsoever on the testimony Proctor attempts to make to
the court, Parris mentions them to shed doubt on Proctor's character. It is a desperate attempt to hold on to the power he has
achieved through the proceedings. Parris becomes increasingly
malicious and unbalanced as the act continues.

Hale, however, has begun to turn around. He is beginning to
see the error of his earlier judgments and now attempts to allow
the truth to be heard. As Act Three progresses, Hale will become
further shaken by the injustice of the hearings until he finally denounces them. At this early point in his transformation, however,
it is already clear that he has lost his influence with the court. He is
all but ignored by Danforth and Hathorne. His revelation has come
too late.

Study Questions

1. What is the significance of lighting described in the stage
   directions?

2. Who is being charged as Act Three begins?

3. What possible motive does Giles Corey offer for the accusations against his wife and others?

4. How are these charges received?

5. Why does Giles feel guilty?

6. What do Proctor and Mary Warren bring with them as
   evidence?

7. How does Judge Danforth measure his worth?

8. What does Parris do when Proctor attempts to make his case?

9. What is happening to Hale at this point?

10. How is Mary's statement that the accusations are mere pre-
    tense received?

Answers

1. The shafts of light entering the room are symbolic of goodness.

2. Martha Corey is being charged as the act begins.

3. Giles Corey accuses Thomas Putnam of attempting to acquire more land.

4. Giles Corey is thrown out of the courtroom and threatened with arrest for contempt.

5. Giles believes he has jeopardized his wife by mentioning that she reads books.

6. They bring a deposition signed by Mary that the trials are a fraud.

7. Judge Danforth measures his worth by the number of people he has jailed and sentenced to hang.

8. Parris attempts to call his Christian character into question.

9. Hale has started to believe that the truth is not being served.

10. The judges believe that the whole group is attempting to undermine the authority of the court by making charges of fraud.

Suggested Essay Topics

1. How do the stage directions add to the understanding of the themes of the play?

2. Some critics have called Judge Danforth a "cardboard villain," too unrelentingly evil to be believed. Is this a fair assessment of the character?

Scene II: Mary Warren's Deposition

Summary

As Danforth considers the claim, he tells Proctor that his wife asserts she is pregnant. The men at first suspect Elizabeth has said this to prevent hanging. John, however, insists that Elizabeth would never lie. On this basis, Danforth offers to let Elizabeth go free until she has delivered. Even so, John cannot in good conscience drop his charge of fraudulence against the court. Danforth reads a deposition stating the good characters of Elizabeth, Rebecca, and Martha, which has been signed by 91 landholding Salem farmers. He then orders all 91 arrested for examination by the court.

Giles Corey has also written a deposition accusing Putnam of having his daughter cry witchery against George Jacobs, who is now jailed. If Jacobs is found to be a witch, he must, by law, give up his property. Putnam is brought in and denounces the accusation as a lie. As doubt is placed on the proceedings, Danforth becomes more adamant in his assertion that the innocent have nothing to fear in the court.

Proctor again presents Mary Warren's deposition, which states that "she never saw Satan; nor any spirit, vague or clear, that Satan may have sent to hurt her. And she declares her friends are lying now." At this point, realizing the seriousness of the statement, Hale suggests that Proctor return with a lawyer to present this claim. Hale has begun to see how uncertain the evidence is against those who have been condemned to die. Danforth retorts that there is no need for a lawyer, since witchcraft is an invisible crime that can have no witnesses other than the victim and the witch.

Analysis

Elizabeth's claim that she is pregnant brings the theme of truth to the foreground of the play. Elizabeth is one of the beacons of truth that has not been overcome by the darkness of the lying all around her. Proctor insists, "if she say she is pregnant, then she

must be! That woman will never lie, Mr. Danforth." For all the cold-ness and disappointment of the Proctor's relationship, Elizabeth's honesty is unquestioned by her husband. Elizabeth's unfailing honesty is sharply contrasted with John's original unwillingness to let the truth be known to the court.

Elizabeth's pregnancy presents John with a decision. Danforth offers to let her live another year and have the child. The offer will save her life; however, in making the offer, Danforth is asking him to give up any further attempt to show that the proceedings are fraudulent. Proctor must again make the difficult decision to ei-ther remain uninvolved or do what he can to make the truth known. Admirably, he chooses to fight for the truth and thus recognizes his responsibility to the society of which he is a part.

Danforth states that "no uncorrupted man may fear this court." We have, however, just witnessed several uncorrupted men at-tempting to present evidence to the court and being charged with contempt. The ridiculousness of this behavior is magnified when all 91 people who signed the deposition in favor of Elizabeth, Martha, and Rebecca are arrested for questioning. Their crime was to attest to the virtue of three upstanding citizens of the commu-nity. As Danforth puts it, "a person is either with this court or he must be counted against it, there be no road between." Being with the court, in this case, means closing one's mind to the evidence of reason and submitting to the mass hysteria that has stopped all business in Salem, save for the trials. No wonder the vast majority of citizens in Salem are afraid to speak against the proceedings. The innocent do, indeed, have much to fear.

Corey's deposition accusing Putnam of "killing his neighbors for their land," shows just how difficult it is to prove what moti-vates anyone. When Putnam soundly denounces the accusation as a lie, it is his word against Corey's. While Putnam conveniently uses the machinery of the court to further his own ends, Corey is challenging the system with thoughts they prefer not to entertain. Just as there is no definitive proof of witchcraft, there can be no definitive proof that Putnam is responsible for charging innocent people.

Hale's assertion that Proctor should return to the court with a lawyer to present his evidence properly shows that he has growing sympathies for the charges of fraud. When he first interrogated

Proctor in his home, there was no room for any evidence save the condition of Proctor's soul. He wholeheartedly assumed that he could make a sound judgment based on his Christian character alone. Now, however, he is beginning to see that the truth of the matter is beyond the scope of such issues as knowing the catechism and plowing on Sunday. He recommends that Proctor get a lawyer to protect him from the unreasonable judgments of Danforth. Where Hale had once been suspicious of the Proctors, he is now attempting to help them. Danforth's assertion that there is no need for lawyers shows how far from actual justice the court has strayed.

Study Questions

1. What news does Danforth give John Proctor about his wife?

2. Why did the court not believe this assertion at first?

3. What does Proctor tell Danforth about his doubts?

4. What offer is made to Proctor by Danforth?

5. What happens to the people who signed the deposition upholding the three women?

6. What does Giles Corey charge in his deposition against Thomas Putnam?

7. How does Putnam answer, and who is believed?

8. What does Mary Warren's deposition claim?

9. What does Hale suggest after the deposition is read?

10. Why does Danforth not allow Proctor to obtain a lawyer?

Answers

1. Proctor is told that his wife claims she is pregnant.

2. The court first assumed that Elizabeth was lying about pregnancy to avoid hanging.

3. Proctor tells Danforth that Elizabeth is incapable of telling a lie.

4. Danforth offers to Elizabeth one year to bear her child, hoping that this will allow him to drop his charges against the court.

5. All 91 signers are ordered arrested for questioning.

6. Corey charges Putnam with attempting to kill his neighbors in order to buy their land.

7. Putnam claims the accusation is a lie, and since the charge cannot be proved, Putnam is believed.

8. Mary's deposition claims she never dealt with Satan and that her friends are lying.

9. Hale advises Proctor to return to the court with a lawyer to present such serious evidence.

10. Danforth claims that the evidence against those accused is invisible and that a lawyer would only call extraneous witnesses.

Suggested Essay Topics

1. What is Giles Corey's role in the play?

2. Examine Elizabeth Proctor as a symbol of truth. How has her husband "paid for" this truthfulness?

Scene III: Abigail's Rebuttal

Summary

Danforth studies the deposition and calls for the other girls to be brought in for questioning. Mary, meanwhile, is questioned by the judge and asserts several times that she has lied in court. Susanna Walcott, Mercy Lewis, Betty Parris, and Abigail are led into the room and told of Mary's confession. Abigail, asked if there is any truth to it, flatly denies it. As Abigail calmly refutes all of Mary's assertions, her character is called into question by Proctor, who tells the others that she has led the girls to dance naked in the woods. Parris is forced to admit that he discovered them dancing. Mary is then asked to fake fainting, as she says she did in the courtroom. She is unable to comply.

When Abby is questioned again, she turns against Mary, claiming that the girl has sent her spirit out. The other girls react likewise. Proctor, in his anger and desperation, grabs Abby and calls her a whore. He then admits that he has had an affair with her and that his wife put her out of their house for being a harlot. Elizabeth is called in to corroborate the story; however, she senses that what she says will have profound consequences for her husband. Elizabeth, not knowing that John has confessed, and allowed no help from him, is torn. When forced to answer directly if John is a lecher, she denies it to save his name. John now stands accused of falsehood.

Hale has been completely won over to John's side and denounces Abby. Abby responds by pointing to the ceiling and claiming she sees a bird there that wishes to tear her face. She accuses Mary of envy. Then the girls begin to mimic all of Mary's words as she frantically begs them to stop pretending. Caught between the desire to tell the truth and the fear of hanging, Mary finally sides with the other girls and accuses Proctor of doing devil's work and of attempting to overthrow the court. The curtain falls as both John Proctor and Giles Corey are taken away to jail.

Analysis

When Abby is confronted with Mary's confession of pretense, we see another case of one person's word against another's. Neither girl's assertions can be proved definitively, one way or another. Frustrated by his failure to convince with reason alone, Proctor realizes that the only way to promote the truth is to play the judge's own game. He therefore begins to illuminate weaknesses in Abby's Christian character. She laughs during prayer; she dances naked in the woods. From these offenses against Puritanism, Proctor hopes to show that Abby is not above lying in the courtroom, and, worse yet, scheming to murder those accused of witchcraft.

Parris reacts to these charges against his niece in a curious way. Rather than defend Abigail, he immediately defends himself. "Excellency, since I come to Salem this man is blackening my name." Parris' involvement in the proceedings has been exclusively to protect his own reputation; his own good name. His paranoia leads him to imagine insults where none are intended. Although in Act One Parris told Abby he thought he saw one of the girls naked, here he flatly denies it. He is less interested in telling the truth than in keeping any wrongdoing of his niece's from surfacing.

Mary Warren, the weakest of the girls and the most likely to be intimidated, finds she cannot stand up to the power of Abigail. Despite Proctor's reassurance that no harm will come to those who tell the truth, she is deathly afraid of Abby. Having been one of the accusers of the court, Mary witnessed many sentences of death by hanging. When Abby turns against her and accuses her of sending her spirit out, she knows what will become of her. She lacks the courage and the strength necessary to be an individual against a powerful majority.

When Proctor sees Mary falter, he uses the one weapon he still holds. He admits to his lechery and surrenders his good name. Proctor gives up his good reputation in Salem to stand up for what he believes is right. He has finally become fully committed to the truth. Elizabeth, the very model of truth, believes she can save her husband by lying. The woman who cannot lie tells a lie. She was doomed either way. To tell the truth was to ruin her husband's good name. To lie was to condemn him. In going against her own na-

ture, her own individuality, Elizabeth begins the sequence that will lead to her husband's death.

Ironically, the one member of the community who tried so hard to remain uninvolved in the witch-hunt has become its central focus. This is a turning point in the play. Proctor, the principle enemy of the witch-hunt, has become its ultimate victim. He is dangerous to the proceedings precisely because he does not believe in them. In order for the epidemic to continue, Proctor must be removed.

The sequence is also climactic for Hale. By the end of Act Three Hale has completely denounced the hearings. Shaken by the injustice that he sees before him, he tries to right the wrong. By this point, however, he has no influence. Danforth tells him "I will have nothing from you, Mr. Hale!" Danforth, while close to perceiving the truth, has no epiphany. Faced with truths and lies, he is unable or unwilling to distinguish between them.

Study Questions

1. What does Abigail do when confronted with Mary's accusation of pretense?

2. What behavior of Abby's does Proctor bring to the judges' attention?

3. Why does he choose to reveal these things?

4. What is Reverend Parris' reaction to these charges against his niece?

5. How is Mary asked to prove that the girls were lying?

6. How does Abigail respond to Mary's assertions that the girls were all lying?

7. What does Proctor finally call Abigail?

8. Who is brought in to back up this accusation, and what does she do?

9. How does Mary finally respond to Abby's behavior?

10. What happens to Proctor at the end of the act?

Answers

1. Abby denies the proceedings are mere pretense.

2. Abby has laughed at prayer and danced naked in the woods.

3. Proctor attempts to show flaws in Abby's Christian character that might prove that she is lying.

4. Parris reacts to the charges against Abby as if they were personal insults against himself.

5. Mary is asked to fake fainting to show how the girls were faking in the court.

6. Abigail turns against Mary, claiming that Mary has sent her spirit out to afflict her.

7. In desperation, Proctor calls Abigail a whore, confessing his lechery.

8. Elizabeth is brought in to back up her husband's testimony, and she lies.

9. Mary is terrified, and rather than risk being hanged as a witch, she once again sides with the other girls and accuses Proctor of being a witch.

10. Proctor is arrested and jailed as a witch.

Suggested Essay Topics

1. What motivates Elizabeth to lie? Is a good name more important than the truth?

2. How is Mary Warren used by both sides? Does she have an individual identity?

Act IV

Scene I: Reverend Parris' Doubts

New Characters:

Sarah Good: *an old beggar woman of Salem accused of witchcraft*

Hopkins: *a prison guard*

Summary

Act Four is set in a cell at the Salem jail the following fall. Sarah Good lies sleeping on one bench, and Tituba on another. Marshal Herrick enters and wakes them, ordering them to move to another cell. Both women carry on about how the devil is coming to fly with them to Barbados.

Deputy Governor Danforth and Judge Hathorne enter, followed by Cheever. From their talk it is apparent that there will be hangings the following day and that Reverend Hale is in the prison praying with those who are to hang. As Herrick is sent to fetch Parris, the other men discuss the minister's odd behavior. He seems to have gone a bit mad, and when he enters it is apparent that he is gaunt and frightened. Parris summoned the two judges back to Salem because his niece, Abigail, and Mercy Lewis have vanished

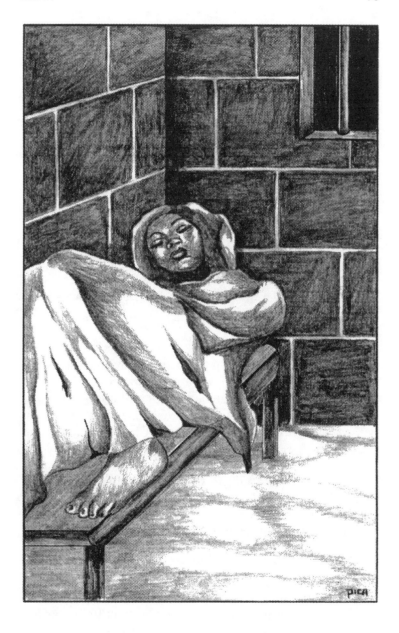

after robbing him of all of his money. Parris believes the girls may have been frightened by the rumors of the rebellion in Andover against the court. Apparently, during a similar situation in Andover, the town banded together and threw out the court, saying they wanted no part of witchcraft.

While the hangings in Salem have gone smoothly so far, Parris fears that the hanging of Rebecca Nurse and John Proctor the next morning will change public sentiment. Unlike the others who have hung, these two are good people who hold great weight in Salem. Parris argues for postponement to give Hale a chance to bring more of the condemned to confess. Danforth denies any postponement. At this denial, Parris reveals that his life has been threatened. He fears physical retaliation if these two die.

Hale has failed to move any of the prisoners to confession. Both Hale and Parris argue for pardon or postponement of the hangings. Danforth refuses to reconsider on the grounds that he will look indecisive and it would be unfair to those who have already hung.

Analysis

Act Four takes place in the Salem jail, dimly lit by moonlight seeping through the bars. The light of goodness is still present, though it has been greatly dimmed. No longer the bright sunlight of Act Three, we now see only the reflected light of the moon. While evil has managed to overpower good, as is vividly portrayed in the apparent madness of Tituba and Sarah Good, it cannot be obliterated.

Tituba represents a distinctly different cultural view of the devil. In her native Barbados, the devil is not seen as the embodiment of evil as he is in Puritan theology. Occult practices were, and still are, accepted in many of the islands. The contrast is between the hatred of differentness exhibited by the Puritans, and the acceptance of diversity seen in the island culture. To Tituba, the devil is not wicked. She says "Devil, him be pleasureman in Barbados, him be singin' and dancin' in Barbados." Where Tituba herself stands on the issue is unclear. The mad ravings of Tituba and Sarah Good are more a reaction against the rigid Puritanism that has condemned them than an embrace of the devil. They have been in jail for many months and are reacting to their circumstances.

Time has passed since Act Three, and it is now fall. The symbolism of the season is apparent. Fall is the time of fruition, when crops reach their fullness and are harvested. It also heralds a time of death and decay. The hysteria of the witch trials has now reached its peak and is approaching its inevitable end. For months the residents of Salem have done nothing but attend the proceedings of the court. There is a real sense that the town is tiring of the spectacle.

Tituba and Sarah Good's madness is mirrored in the madness of Reverend Parris. He has been reduced to a shadow of the man in Act One, gaunt, frightened, and prone to sudden weeping. Parris has summoned the judges back to Salem to discuss the disappearance of his niece, Abigail, and Mercy Lewis with all of his money. While nothing to this point had convinced Parris of the error of his ways, the loss of his money seems to have awakened him to the significance of the court's actions. The rumors of Andover have also begun to turn public opinion, and alliance with the witch-hunt is no longer politically advantageous for the minister. He begins to argue for postponement of the hangings in order to bring more of the condemned to confess and save their lives.

The situation in Andover is crucial. Apparently, a similar court set up there to condemn witches was thrown out by the people of the town who rebelled against its authority. Danforth attempts to silence any talk about the rebellion; however, the news has already spread through Salem. The rumor spread in this act parallels the rumors of witchcraft spread in the beginning of the play. Just as the earlier rumors quickly took hold of the town and led to the witch hysteria, so Danforth fears these new rumors will quickly undermine his authority. The disappearance of Abigail and Mercy Lewis after the Andover rebellion casts serious doubt on their testimony.

Parris fears that the hanging of two such upstanding citizens as Rebecca Nurse and John Proctor the next morning will incite a rebellion in Salem similar to the one in Andover. Still, Danforth refuses to budge. The reason he gives is that "postponement now speaks of floundering on my part." He is not so much concerned about the lives of those condemned as about his own reputation. He does not wish to appear weak, opening himself up to criticism of the entire proceeding. Once again, the ends justify the means.

Miller himself has said of Danforth "there are people dedicated to evil in the world; that without their perverse example we should not know the good." While it may have been possible to excuse Danforth's earlier behavior as a necessary result of the authority he holds, this refusal to examine his actions for fear of losing face is abominable.

Hale has now come full circle in his development. While he appeared in Salem bearing the weighty authority of his books on the devil and witchcraft, he is now there to attempt to reverse the consequences of that early behavior. Far from examining the souls of these men and women and judging their content, he is now encouraging them to lie and save their lives. Hale is finally acting as an individual, and he attempts to persuade others to do the same. The trials had been a farce, and Hale saw no sin in telling a lie to an unjust authority to save one's life. As Hale was fanatical in his zeal to find witches, he is now fanatical in his zeal to save lives. His argument that the victims should all be pardoned is greatly weakened by the fact that at least one of those condemned has already confessed. Danforth will no longer take him seriously. His efforts are too late.

Study Questions

1. What are Tituba and Sarah Good discussing as the act opens?

2. How does Tituba describe the devil in Barbados?

3. What has happened that has made Parris so anxious?

4. What happened in Andover?

5. Why is Parris afraid to hang John Proctor and Rebecca Nurse the next morning?

6. Why is Parris more frightened to hang Proctor and Nurse than anyone else?

7. Why does Parris request a postponement of the hangings?

8. What does Hale request instead of postponement?

9. Why does Danforth refuse Hale's request?

10. What has Hale been advising those condemned to do?

Answers

1. The two women are speaking of the devil coming to take them back to Barbados.

2. Tituba says the devil is a "pleasureman" in Barbados, a joyful figure.

3. Abigail and Mercy Lewis have run off with all of the minister's money.

4. A court examining witches in Andover was overturned and rejected by the town.

5. Parris fears a rebellion in Salem similar to the one in Andover.

6. Proctor and Nurse are well respected in Salem and have far better reputations than any of those previously put to death.

7. Parris hopes that more of those condemned can be brought to confess and save their lives.

8. Because none of the prisoners can be brought to confess, Hale requests a pardon.

9. Danforth refuses to pardon anyone on the grounds that he will appear to be wavering in his judgment and that it is not fair to the 12 who have already hung.

10. Hale advises the prisoners to lie and save their lives.

Suggested Essay Topics

1. Has Parris experienced moral development or is he merely attempting to stay on the right side of public opinion?

2. How is Tituba's understanding of the devil different from that of most citizens of Salem?

Scene II: Elizabeth and John Contemplate Confession

Summary

The judges decide to bring John and Elizabeth together, hoping that his pregnant wife will soften John's resolve. When Elizabeth arrives, Hale pleads with her to convince her husband to confess and save his life. John is dragged in and the two are left alone.

Elizabeth reveals that a hundred or more of the accused have confessed and gone free. The two weigh the merits of confession against the value of remaining in the truth. When Hathorne returns for his answer, John asserts that he wants his life. As Hathorne cries out the news, John immediately doubts his decision, struggling with the evil of the lie.

Analysis

By this point, Hale's attempts to rectify the wrongs done to those condemned has reached near hysteria. He has again let his emotion overpower his principle, this time in the very opposite extreme. He is attempting to convince the prisoners that two wrongs will make a right. As he himself says, "I come to do the Devil's work. I come to counsel Christians they should belie themselves." His assertion that "there is blood on my head! Can you not see the blood on my head!" mimics Lady Macbeth as she attempts to wash her bloodstained hands in Shakespeare's *Macbeth*. Hale tells Elizabeth "I would save your husband's life, for if he is taken I count myself his murderer." The extent of the guilt that he feels is enormous.

The short scene between Elizabeth and John Proctor in the jail is pivotal to the play. Hale counsels Elizabeth to convince her husband to lie. Elizabeth, however, has seen the results of her own lie, which led to John's sentence to death. Her calmness in the face of tragedy astounds Danforth. The emotion between husband and wife at first laying eyes on each other is powerful. Each had

sacrificed to save the other: John by offering up his reputation; Elizabeth by lying. Both attempts were a dismal failure. John's death is just hours away.

John Proctor's choice does not come as easily as Rebecca Nurse's. His good name—his identity—is crucial to him. If he joins the mistaken majority and admits witchcraft, he will lose his identity. This is a much deeper concept of a good name than mere reputation. The confession of his relationship with Abigail was about his standing in the eyes of others. This confession will be about his own personal integrity. Proctor's name is threatened only by his fear of death and the knowledge of his own adultery. What the community thinks of him is not his concern. His concern is to be true to himself. To confess is to be a fraud.

Of course, to confess is also to save his life. Is it true, as Hale insists, that "life is God's most precious gift" and that "no principle, however glorious, may justify the taking of it"? Elizabeth would say it is not. To her the goal should not be life at any price, but a life of moral integrity. To confess is too great a concession. Curiously, Proctor struggles not with the telling of the lie that will save his life, but with the image he will present if he chooses to die. He knows that Rebecca Nurse will be seen, deservedly, as a martyr. He feels that he has not earned such a death; he is unworthy of that appellation. Proctor has not lived up to his own moral standards. The calm demeanor of his wife only serves to emphasize his unworthiness. He is tempted to agree with Hale and avoid a meaningless death.

Proctor has decided to sign a confession; however, he is not secure in his decision, and he seeks the approval of his wife. He admits that he has only waited this long because "it is hard to give a lie to dogs." Elizabeth withholds her advice. She thinks this decision must be made by John deeply searching his own conscience. Elizabeth has changed. She has seen her coldness and the reasons for John's adultery. She has realized that neither she nor any other person on earth can be his judge. Her statement that "whatever you will do, it is a good man does it" is a long way from comments in Act Two. Elizabeth has not attempted to sway him, and John delivers his decision: he will have his life.

Study Questions

1. What does Hale plead with Elizabeth to do?
2. Why does Hale believe a lie would not be a sin in this case?
3. Why is Hale so adamant in his attempts to convince Elizabeth?
4. Have any of the other prisoners confessed?
5. What reason does John give for not confessing?
6. What further reason keeps John from confessing?
7. What has John decided to do before he sees Elizabeth?
8. What does Elizabeth advise him to do?
9. How has Elizabeth changed?
10. What reason does John have for not telling the truth and going to his death?

Answers

1. Hale pleads with Elizabeth to convince John to lie.
2. Hale believes that no principle can justify the taking of a life.
3. Hale feels he will be responsible for John's death.
4. Elizabeth tells John that a hundred or more people have confessed and gone free.
5. John states that he does not want to give a lie to dogs.
6. To confess is to go along with the majority and give up his individual identity.
7. John has decided to confess when he meets with Elizabeth.
8. Elizabeth will not advise him either way. She knows he must decide for himself.
9. Elizabeth has realized that she, too, is at fault and that she cannot be John's judge.
10. John feels unworthy to die the death of a martyr since he has not lived up to his own moral standard.

Suggested Essay Topics

1. How is the conversation between husband and wife in this scene different from the opening scene of Act Two?

2. Elizabeth will not give her advice to John, but how does she influence him?

Scene III: John Proctor's Decision

Summary

The others reenter the cell, and Cheever prepares to take a statement. John begins to answer the questions put to him, agreeing that he saw the devil and that he did the devil's work on the earth. Soon after the formal confession is begun, however, Rebecca Nurse is brought in to witness it in the hope that it will, in turn, cause her own confession. Rebecca is astonished that John would do such a thing. When John is pressed to name those he has seen with the devil, he refuses to taint their good names. Danforth finally asks him to sign his confession and he at first refuses, then signs. Afterward, however, he snatches up the paper and refuses to give it back to be posted on the door of the church.

At this point, John begins to act irrationally. He believes he has confessed before God and that there is no need for the piece of paper bearing his signature. If it is posted, he knows he will cast doubt on the innocence of those who refuse to confess and are hanged. He finally breaks down and tells Danforth he has signed his name to a lie. As Danforth asks one last time for the paper, John tears it up and crumples it. He has found the resolve to stand by the truth and to hang for it. Rebecca and John are led out to their deaths, while Hale and Parris plead with Elizabeth to attempt to sway her husband's decision. The play ends with the final statement from Elizabeth: "He have his goodness now. God forbid I take it from him!"

Analysis

The theme of the good name is critically important in this last scene of the play. While Proctor verbally confesses to witchcraft, he refuses to name others who are involved. He is refusing to spoil anyone's good name or reputation in the community. Proctor realizes that one's name is everything. His refusal is taken as a sign that he is not truly repentant. Of course he is not repentant. He has done nothing wrong; however, slandering the names of others is perversely seen as a sign of rightness with God.

Proctor, after much protest, proceeds to sign a written confession. He refuses, however, to surrender it to the judge. The written evidence of his dishonesty is more than he can bear. Proctor also knows that his signature will be posted publicly on the church doors and used to force others to confess, thereby losing their own identities. He refuses to incriminate others or to serve as an example of submission. It is enough that he has offered the lie. God knows his soul and should be its only judge. The reason that he gives to Danforth in the climax of the play comes back to the idea of a good name: "Because it is my name! . . . How may I live without my name? I have given you my soul; leave me my name!"

Proctor finally asserts his individuality and claims his name by denouncing his confession as a lie. In a vivid gesture, he tears and crumples the paper before the judges. Proctor is honest, above all, with himself. To confess is to align himself with what he believes to be evil. The prosecution is the real example of the devil. All who consort with them, then, become true witches. For Proctor, to confess is to admit the truth of the court's charge against him. In the end he refuses to surrender his unique beliefs. He makes the choice that costs him his life but restores his soul. Proctor surprises himself with this new strength. "You have made your magic now," he says, "for now I do think I see some shred of goodness in John Proctor." Proctor has earned his death in his final act. His achievement is heralded by his wife, who says to Hale: "He have his goodness now. God forbid I take it from him!"

Miller has stated that he was drawn to this subject by the "moral size" of the people involved. "They knew who they were." Each of the 20 who died in Salem believed so strongly in themselves and in the rightness of their consciences as to die rather than belie themselves. In a situation where "men were handing their conscience to other men and thanking them for the opportunity to do so," they refused to give in. While the parallel to the McCarthy era is striking, the lessons of the play are applicable to any situation that allows the accuser to be always right. It is similarly applicable to any conflict between the individual and authority. The final authority must always rest not with the majority, but with the individual conscience.

Study Questions

1. Why is Rebecca Nurse brought in to witness Proctor's confession?

2. Why does Proctor refuse to name the names of other witches?

3. Why does Proctor refuse to give Danforth the paper with his signature on it?

4. What is the climax of the play?

5. What does Proctor do with the signed confession?

6. How has Proctor earned his death?

7. How does Elizabeth react to his choice of death?

8. When does Proctor claim his good name?

9. What reaction does Rebecca Nurse have to John Proctor's confession?

10. Does Rebecca Nurse confess?

Answers

1. It is hoped that Proctor's confession will lead Rebecca to confess as well.

2. While Proctor has made his own decision, he refuses to ruin anyone else's good name.

3. He does not want it used to force others to confess or be seen as an example of submission.

4. The climax of the play is Proctor's assertion that his confession was a lie.

5. Proctor tears and crumples the signed confession in front of the judges.

6. Proctor has earned his death by asserting his individuality against the authority of the court.

7. Elizabeth is proud that John has found his goodness and refuses to dissuade him.

8. Proctor finds his good name when he asserts his individuality and tears up his confession.

9. Rebecca is shocked by Proctor's confession.

10. Rebecca refuses to belie herself by making a false confession.

Suggested Essay Topics

1. How would Proctor be saving his good name no matter which choice he made? Why does he choose as he does?

2. Some critics find it hard to believe Proctor's choice of death. Discuss his decision based on his relationships with other characters throughout the play.

Sample Analytical Paper Topics

The following paper topics are based on the entire play. Following each topic is a thesis and sample outline. Use these as a starting point for your paper.

Topic #1

One of the most prominent themes in *The Crucible* is the importance of a good name. Analyze what a good name means to several of the characters, using specific examples to support your conclusions.

Outline

I   Thesis Statement: *One central motif of* The Crucible *is the importance of a good name. The meaning of a good name to John Proctor at the end of the play, however, is vastly different from the good name that Reverend Parris seeks.*

II.   A good name as pride and reputation

   A.   Reverend Parris

   B.   Judge Danforth

III. A good name as goodness

   A.   Rebecca Nurse

   B.   Elizabeth Proctor

IV.   A good name as individuality and moral integrity

    A.   John Proctor

    B.   Reverend Hale

V.   The naming of names

Topic #2

The Crucible is vitally concerned with the presentation of truth. Show how truth is portrayed in the play and how various characters show their true natures.

Outline

I.   Thesis Statement: *The judges of Salem are not concerned with seeking the truth and justice, but with maintaining their authority and reputations. This goal leads them to consistently reject truth, against all logic and evidence of their senses.*

II.   Symbols of truth

    A.   Elizabeth Proctor

    B.   Rebecca Nurse

    C.   John Proctor

III. Symbols of falsehood

    A.   Reverend Parris

    B.   Abigail

IV.   Hale's reaction to the truth

    A.   On first arriving in Salem

    B.   At the end of the play

V.   Danforth's reaction to the truth

    A.   Giles Corey's evidence

    B.   Mary Warren's confession

    C.   John Proctor's reason

Topic #3

There are many examples of authority in *The Crucible*. It is tempting for a contemporary reader to accept John Proctor's choice of following only the authority of his conscience, but whose response does *The Crucible* support as the true model of authority?

Outline

I.   Thesis Statement: *While authority stems from many different sources and is responded to in many ways,* The Crucible *supports the response of Rebecca Nurse as the true model.*

II. The authority of the written word

    A.   The Bible

    B.   Hale's books on witchcraft

III. The authority of the church leaders

    A.   Reverend Parris

    B.   Reverend Hale

IV. The authority of the court

    A.   Judge Danforth

    B.   Judge Hathorne

V.   The authority of individual conscience

    A.   John Proctor

VI. Rebecca Nurse's response

    A.   Respect for outward authority

    B.   True to her conscience

SECTION SEVEN

Bibliography

All quotations in this MAXnotes edition were taken from the Penguin edition of the play, New York, 1981.

Douglass, James W., "Miller's *The Crucible:* Which Witch Is Which?" in *Renascence*, vol. xv, no. 3, Spring, 1963, pp. 145–151.

Griffin, John and Griffin, Alice, "Arthur Miller Discusses *The Crucible*," in Theatre Arts, vol. xxxcii, no. 10, October, 1953, pp. 33–34.

Hewes, Henry, "Arthur Miller and How He Went to the Devil," in *The Saturday Review*, New York, vol. xxxvi, no. 5, January 31, 1953, pp. 24–26.

Hill, Philip G., "*The Crucible*: A Structural View," in *Modern Drama*, vol. 10, no. 3, December, 1967, pp. 312–317.

Hope-Wallace, Philip, in a review of *The Crucible* in *Time & Tide*, vol. 35, no. 47, November 20, 1954, p. 1544.

Huftel, Sheila, *Arthur Miller: The Burning Glass*, The Citadel Press, 1965.

Introduction to *Arthur Miller's Collected Plays*, The Viking Press, 1957, pp. 3–55.

"Journey to *The Crucible*," in *The New York Times*, February 8, 1953, section 10, p. 3.

Miller, Arthur, in an interview with Matthew C. Roudane in *Michigan Quarterly Review*, Summer, 1985.

Popkin, Henry, "Arthur Miller's *The Crucible*," in *College English*, vol. 26, no. 2, November, 1964, pp. 139–146.

Raphael, D.D., *The Paradox of Tragedy: The Mahlon Powell Lectures, 1959*, Indiana University Press, 1960, pp. 90–111.

Warshow, Robert, *The Immediate Experience*, Doubleday & Company, Inc., 1962, pp. 189–203.

Welland, Dennis, *Arthur Miller*, Oliver and Boyd Ltd., 1961.

Available at your local bookstore or order directly from us by sending in coupon below.

MAXnotes® are simply the best – but don't just take our word for it...

"... I have told every bookstore in the area to carry your MAXnotes. They are the only notes I recommend to my students. There is no comparison between MAXnotes and all other notes ..."
  – *High School Teacher & Reading Specialist,*
  Arlington High School, Arlington, MA

"... I discovered the MAXnotes when a friend loaned me her copy of the *MAXnotes for Romeo and Juliet.* The book really helped me understand the story. Please send me a list of stores in my area that carry the MAXnotes. I would like to use more of them ..."
  – *Student, San Marino, CA*

"... The two MAXnotes titles that I have used have been very, very useful in helping me understand the subject matter reviewed. Thank you for creating the MAXnotes series ..."
  – *Student, Morrisville, PA*

"...These notes really helped me study! I don't know what I would have done without them!..."
  – *Student, Philadelphia, PA*